Mike & Linda —
Blessings of
you serve
Gal 6: 14

MW00439659

ALL THE WAY
HOME

Bruce Snavely

ALL THE WAY HOME

Copyright © 2014 by Bruce Snavely

Globalmax Publications

ISBN: 978-0615974811

Cover Design by Mike Zizolfo

To Grace and our children, Allison, Amy, Ashley, and Johnathan — my home.

"Be still, sad heart! and cease repining;
Behind the clouds is the sun still shining;
Thy fate is the common fate of all,
Into each life some rain must fall"

— Henry Wadsworth Longfellow

PROLOGUE

Home defines who you are, but however home may be defined, its essence isn't the brick and mortar which closes you in but the love, acceptance, and self-affirmation which one day sets you free to leave it. I had that once when I was very young, but then it all seemed to vanish almost as quickly as it had appeared.

For the next several years, I held out for the home and the love I would never get back. Perhaps Providence never intended to return things to the way they once were, yet the idea of home was something I was blindly determined to rediscover. Before that day would ever arrive, my life and my brother's would unravel into hopelessness while my sister would become a victim of a brutal and sadistic serial killer.

This is the story of how at least one of us finally made it —*all the way home*.

CHAPTER ONE

Ivy League Beginnings

HOME, FOR ME, began with the family that eventually brought me into the world. My dad's family had come to settle in Massillon, Ohio where my grandfather, John Snavely taught high school math and coached the local high school football team. John, who had a glass eye and went by the name of Jack, coached the first undefeated team in Massillon, Ohio in 1919. He would be followed there by the better-known Paul Brown of Cleveland Browns' fame.

In the twenties, Granddad was invited to Shaw High School in Cleveland, which was a prestigious and well respected football school. My dad and both his younger brothers Bill and Jim played at Shaw for their father. Dad starred at quarterback and about everything else he did. Early in life, his mother, a concert pianist, had instilled in him a love for music. She died when he was fifteen, but her influence in music would affect him for the rest of his life. After finishing high school in 1935, he was accepted at Yale and played offensive guard on the

Iron Man teams from 1935-1937.

Dad married his high school sweetheart, Betsy, while doing his undergraduate work at Yale. They had four children, and times were tough. It was during the Depression, and education—like everything else, during this time in America—was not available to everybody. His daughter Joan, my half-sister, told me once that Dad had made a hundred-dollar bet with a teammate from New Jersey that he could finish the four-year undergrad program in three. During the depression, that was like a thousand dollars because nobody had any money. Being blessed with a brilliant mind and his share of determination, he won the bet. He was accepted into the medical school at Yale in the fall of 1938, just a year before Hitler invaded Poland to start the Second World War. I was told that Dad did two things on the side to pay his way through college. First, he started a jazz band. They played weekends in New Haven and New York, and eventually he became the director of the Connecticut Colonials' staff orchestra for WICC in New Haven in 1940. Second, he ran a small corner store below his apartment near the campus. Betsy ran the store while dad studied. Between both extracurricular activities, they paid the bills and raised the kids, but Dad and Betsy's relationship had fallen on hard times.

By the mid forties, he went to work in the pathology department at St. Luke's Hospital in Cleveland while completing his medical internship. During his tenure there, he met a young, attractive girl who worked in the medical records department named Lilyan Kovach. In 1944, he divorced Betsy, gave her custody of the four children, and married Lilyan. Her close-knit Hungarian family had warned her not to get involved with him, but fortunately for me, she ignored their advice and married him anyway. As his personal secretary, she was required one day to take stenographic notes on an autopsy he performed. Evidently, he had successfully retrieved the body of a woman just minutes after she had been declared dead by his coroner friend at the hospital. Getting a warm, recently deceased corpse is every pathologist's desire because the tissue is still warm and lifelike. Within minutes he was removing her internal organs, while Lilyan was dutifully taking notes. When he removed the woman's heart, it was evidently still beating, prompting Lilyan to scream, "Jeff, she was still alive!" Actually, she wasn't, but my future mother didn't realize it at the time. She also didn't realize the impact of marrying Jeff Snavely.

After they married in 1944, Jeff and Lilyan moved back to Stamford where they eventually had the first of three children. Lee, my sister, was born in 1950. It was about three years later that dad was hired as the head of pathology in a small hospital in northwest Ohio. He bought an old farm on the outskirts of the small university town of Bowling Green. It was there my brother came along in 1953, and I was born in 1956 in the middle of the baby boom generation. Our farm was fairly large for the mid fifties. It was located about five miles east of town and consisted of about two hundred fifty acres surrounding a small river running through it. There were three houses on the property. The main farm is where we lived at the corner of Dirlam and Napoleon

Roads. A smaller farm lay across the river about a quarter mile down Napoleon Road with yet another smaller house on the north end of the property. We lived in the biggest house, which Dad had remodeled. Later he had an in-ground pool built right between the house and one of our dog kennels. At the rear of the property there were two big barns connected in the middle by a pole-barn. Adjacent to the front barn, he built a three-car garage. He rented out all the farmable acreage to a nearby farmer, but we children had the run of the land. It was paradise for a kid.

Dad had multiple interests in life besides medicine. He loved animals, especially dogs. He bought a sickly male German shepherd from a doctor friend of his and successfully nursed it back to health. The dog was named Kondor, and in the wintertime Kondor would pull my brother and me around on the sled. At one time we had nearly a hundred dogs in the kennels, the puppies of which were all sired by Kondor. He was our housedog and like any German shepherd, he was highly protective of the family. We had a sign right outside the fence to our backyard which read, "Guard Dog On Duty, Please Ring the Bell." As kids, we always thought it was funny when someone forgot to ring the bell and barged in the gate. Kondor would be quietly let out the back door on such occasions. It would usually end all right, but it wasn't very amusing for the negligent visitor desperately trying to climb back over the fence to evade Kondor.

We also had about two-hundred fifty Corriedale sheep along with several horses. Every year the sheep were sheared up at the barn and dad would take blood samples from them for lab tests. Down the road at the smaller property called the "little house," dad kept and maintained several hundred white rats in an insulated outside building. These were also used for laboratory testing. I remember one day dad called from the hospital and instructed my mother to exterminate all the rats. I guess a man had been slightly bitten by one of them and about three days later he dropped over dead. The autopsy indicated death from natural causes, but for safety's sake, the health department required us to dispose of the rats. My mother told Geoff and me to go down to the little house and get started exterminating the rats. As kids, we didn't quite know how to go about it efficiently, so we thought we would execute them one by one. We would take them out of the cage, hold them firmly by the back legs and smash them up against the door jam. It worked after two times or so, but it was painfully slow—not to mention—very inhumane. About an hour after all this my mother appeared, and we then decided to put a couple gallons of ether in a barrel, put all the rats in the barrel and cover it so it was air tight. About an hour later they were all dead, and the job was finished.

We also had a big garden full of raspberries, potatoes, carrots, sweet corn, and tomatoes. At the little house there was a pear tree, an apple tree, and a cherry tree. I can still remember gorging on cherries as a little boy. Despite being a non-religious man, dad's spiritual senses told him that people who ate good, wholesome food, presumably created by God, didn't need to take vitamins. In fact, I got first-hand evidence of that one day. Someone, I don't know who, left a bottle of liquid vitamins on our kitchen counter. Each morning when I woke up, which was always early, I would ask Dad if I could have some vitamins. He would always reply, "Bruce, you don't need to take any vitamins." Unfortunately, I couldn't understand why I couldn't have some, if just a little. So, every day I asked, and every day I got the same answer until this one morning. I said, "Dad, can I have some vitamins today?" Dad replied, "Bring me the bottle and a spoon, Bruce". I thought to myself, "Yea, I won!" My father opened the sealed contents and gave me a spoonful. Not bad, I thought. But before I knew it he gave me another, then another, and another...until finally I had lost count. By the time dad was finished with this object lesson, I truly wanted nothing more to do with vitamins forever. Needless to say, that was the day I was introduced to dad the disciplinarian. When he said something, he meant it.

On the other hand, Dad's firmness had its good side too. I loved fresh tomatoes with a little vinegar and sugar. One day a man came over to our house around lunchtime during the late summer when I was about four or five. I was at the table eating fresh garden tomatoes one slice after another. The visitor promptly told me to stop eating so many or I might get sick. I was about to obey when my dad came in the room and told me I could eat all the tomatoes I cared to eat, and like the vitamin ordeal, he meant it. Dad also kept his word. If he said we were going fishing Saturday night after dinner, we went fishing. Of course, all we had to do was go down to the river and cast in a line, but dad never disappointed us. I remember several times when I would accompany him to the bait shop in town to get night crawlers. He was never impatient with me and seemed to delight in having me with him. Of course, the feeling was always mutual.

On most Friday nights, we usually went out to eat at his favorite steak house, the Bungalow. My mom would always dress us up to the nines. It was a big deal for my brother and me. One time he bought us both brand new cowboy boots and hats. That next Friday night, Dad, Geoff, and I marched into the steak house decked out with all our cowboy gear. I think my father got as big a kick out of it as we did. One evening Dad bought me my first lobster, and that was about the end of my steak eating. As far as I remember I ate lobster every time we went out to the Bungalow after that. On the way home, I would get to sit on his lap and steer his white Thunderbird convertible. Child seats weren't in vogue yet. Oftentimes, Dad would take me along with him to the hospital when I was not in school. I don't know why, but riding in the car with Dad always seemed like an adventure to me. For one thing, it was the only doctor-driven convertible in town equipped with glass packs. It also had electric windows, and I can tell you why I remember them.

One day it was raining, and I was headed into the hospital with him when we passed the university campus. As expected, there were lots of students walking back and forth to class that day, most carrying umbrellas. One problem though. Dad thought that men who carried umbrellas were somehow less than real men. So as we passed the campus that day, he spotted a young, male student with his rain protector, and Dad instructed me to stick my head out the window and call him a sissy as loudly as I could. Well, I have never been bashful, so I thought this would be great fun. Dad, who had control of the windows on his side, drove along close to the victim while I let him have it at the top of my five year-old lungs. Each time he found a ready dupe that day for me to harass, he seemed to laugh louder. By the time we got to the end of that stretch of road along the campus, we were like a rolling circus. You can imagine what this whole scene must have looked like to the casual observer. Thanks to my father, I have always had serious difficulty using umbrellas.

However, my Ivy League dad had another side to him which would affect us kids as much as his sense of fun. After school one night a week, Dad hired a French tutor to teach all three of us a second language. Since I was so young, my brother and sister got most of the serious training. It lasted for about an hour, after which the tutor would test them. The grades were logged like any other normal school, and the instructor would leave the results for my Dad when he got home from the hospital that night. Invariably, dad would come in the door, kiss us all and then ask one straight forward question to my siblings. "What did get on your test today, Lee?" "A", she'd reply, always an A. Then the same question was asked of my brother. Almost just as consistently, Geoff would very hesitantly answer, "D." Seldom did the results vary, or the consequences for that matter. Dad would then instruct Geoff to get a hockey stick from behind the breezeway door, and Dad would apply the business end to Geoff's derriere. I happened to have learned a lot of other French words too, but because of my age, Dad did not hold me quite as accountable for ultimate judgment. As for Geoff, I never could quite figure out after that why he was not more motivated to get his grades up. Unfortunately, he wasn't.

It seemed like Geoff always had the bad stuff happen to him. One day we were helping Bill, the hired hand, haul manure from one of the horse stalls. We each had a pitchfork, and we would fill it up as much as we could carry, and throw the contents into the manure spreader just outside the door. Well, I got tired or distracted first, so I leaned my pitchfork up against the wall by the door. A few minutes went by, and Geoff came out of the stable with a big load on his fork. As he walked by the door to heave it up into the spreader, my pitchfork slid down the wall and went right through his lower leg. As he writhed and screamed on the concrete floor, Bill ran over. Seeing what had happened, he pulled the pitchfork out of Geoff's leg, picked him up and literally sprinted all the way up to the house. I thought I was in trouble since it was my fork that got Geoff. I walked around to the front barn and waited to see what would happen. A few minutes later Dad came out with Geoff. Passing by the barn, he looked in and saw me standing there. He must have known I felt bad about what had happened, but he said nothing, and I felt no blame or hostility from him about the incident. It was just an accident, and that was it. Dad took Geoff into the hospital, cleaned the wound, gave him a shot of penicillin, and about an hour later, they were home and the day continued as normal.

On another occasion, Geoff was out baling hay with

Bill, when he was bit on the finger by a field mouse caught in a hay bale. Once again, Bill brought Geoff to the house. Dad made them go back out to the field and find the mouse. Luckily, they had killed it, and it wasn't that hard to find. Dad took it up to the lab and tested it to see if it was rabid. Fortunately, it wasn't, and all Geoff got out of it was a couple of tiny puncture marks on his finger and the bragging rights of being bitten by a rodent and living to tell about it, heady stuff for an eight year-old.

My fortunes had always seemed a little more Providentially ordered for good. For example, during the first year of my life in 1956, a vicious windstorm went through our area just outside of town. That afternoon, dad was doing something out in the barn while mom was in and out of the house in the back yard. I was in my playpen under the shade of the tree just outside the backdoor when the storm began. I was told later that the storm came up so fast that dad was stuck in the barn while mom was momentarily stuck at the back door. Both were frozen in fear because I was still in the playpen and both were trying to scream to each other over the roar of the wind to get me to safety. Evidently, my mother, who was the closest, got to me and got back in the house before the worst of the winds arrived. Moments later, the shade tree I had been under snapped off and fell directly on the playpen, crushing it. In fact, I somehow ended up with the original picture showing what was left of the tree stump. I had definitely been spared. I learned later in life why that might have been. My half-sister, Joannie, told me that one night before the first divorce in New Haven, that dad had offhandedly announced to her and her brothers, that one of his sons was going to become a minister. Little did Dad know that his youngest son of a second marriage would fulfill his off-handed premonition.

One day Bill, Geoff, and I were out hauling manure early one morning from the back stable. Bill pulled the tractor with the manure spreader into the barnyard and parked it nose first right up by the barn. As we were getting off the tractor with Bill, my mom called us to come in for breakfast. Bill didn't always eat with us, but that morning he came in to have breakfast. As I finished my last bite, I announced to Bill and Geoff that I was going out to start the tractor, and I would be waiting for them to join me. Without hesitation, I ran out to the barnyard where the tractor was parked. Excitedly, I jumped on and nestled myself into the tractor seat, turned the key on, and hit the big green starter button with my foot. I didn't know that Bill had left the tractor in low gear so it wouldn't roll, so when I hit the starter, it came alive and immediately began lurching forward. It had enough throttle to not only keep running but power enough to begin climbing up the barn wall. I didn't know what to do and was just sitting there hanging on to the steering wheel to keep from falling off as it went up the wall. At the point when the tractor could go no further without tipping over backwards, I felt a body climb on top of mine and a big boot hit the clutch backing the tractor back down off the barn. Fortunately, Bill had followed me out of the house. For as long as we lived on the farm, you could see the black tire mark on the side of the front barn. Needless to say, I never tried to start the tractor again without Bill being in the tractor seat. Once again, it seemed that I had been spared.

Ironically, dad always appeared to me to be almost god-like. When he was around, there wasn't a cloud on the horizon. There was never any question in our minds about how much he loved us kids. His affection was always ready and abundant, and he loved to share music with us. I will never forget the old ditty,

"There was an old man named Michael Finnigan, He had whiskers on his chinigan, shave 'em off and they'd grow in again, poor old Michael Finnigan, begin again."

If we wanted he would sit there and play that for my brother and me until we couldn't sing anymore. Sometimes he would break out the accordion and strap it on and play. I remember several weekends when he would have his old jazz buddies from New Haven come down, and they would be playing in the living room until late in the day on Sunday. Having been known as the "Jazz Maestro" during his band days in New Haven, Dad played the piano and the slide trombone equally well.

During the summer months, we spent a lot of time in the pool. Dad taught Geoff and me how to dive for silver dollars. In the evening with the underwater lights on, he would throw a coin in, and we would take turns diving in to retrieve it. If we caught it before it hit bottom, we'd get to keep it and put it in our piggy banks.

These are the things I recollect most about my dad and our memorable days on the farm. For me, life seemed to be almost idyllic. I was growing up in a wealthy doctor's home. I knew and felt love, and my world held no real fears. As dad said of me one time,

"Bruce is bright, healthy, and aggressive." Looking back, I realize that my life was already being laid out before me. Naturally, I would grow up to be just like dad. I would be well educated, probably play football, and likely follow him, along with my two uncles to Yale. And I certainly would never carry an umbrella. But unfortunately, things don't always work out the way they're planned.

CHAPTER TWO

Horse in a Drum

LIKE ANY KID, all my early family memories were not perfect, despite the security we children felt in our family and farm. For one thing, my father was not faithful to my mother. He had not been to his first wife. He had begun the affair with my mother while doing his internship at St. Luke's in Cleveland. His subsequent divorce from Betsy and remarriage to Lilyan in 1944 was as quick as it took to get to Reno and back. This is why my mom's family warned her not to marry Jeff Snavely. But Dad could be very charming and persuasive, and mom's wholesome roots deeply attracted him to her family. They dignified their hurried union for the family with a formal event at the Hungarian Lutheran Church in Cleveland. Now married, they finished dad's internship in Cleveland and returned to Stamford, Connecticut, for dad's first full-time post at the local hospital there. After my sister's birth in 1950 they decided on the big move to northwest Ohio.

By the time my brother and I came along, our family

was complete, and life on the farm with my doctor-dad and mom began. In the mid nineteen fifties the postwar economy was chugging along nicely, and dad was making very good money as a well-established pathologist. He ran two pathology departments and three pathology laboratories in the area. He was gone long hours, and as I learned later, it was not always work that kept him away. As I indicated, he had an enormous proclivity for women. There were always attractive female associates on the hospital side of things, and dad had also hired a pretty little accountant to whom he rented the little house on the north end of our property. All of this obviously did not set well with my mother, and even though we were not always aware of it, tensions often ran high at home.

But this was not the only stress between them. Dad, despite having some deep religious roots coming from his own grandfather, was an avowed agnostic. My mother on the other hand, was raised in a moderate Lutheran home environment in Cleveland. She thought we should all be sent to Sunday school as she had been as a little girl. My dad allowed us to go, but evidently thought little of it. The hired hand would take us there and back. I liked it because he would usually stop at a corner store near the church and buy us bubble-gum cigars to consume on the way home. Consequently for me, Sunday school was just as memorable as catching frogs down at the river.

Unfortunately for us kids, the happy façade did not always stay intact for mom and dad. There were times at the dinner table when I remember dad getting up from the table and telling my mother to go into the living room off the kitchen. There would be arguing and then the unforgettable sounds of physical violence. For my mother, these episodes probably appeared as the fruits of an ill-fated marriage, but to us kids, they were plain, flat unsettling.

To cope with her life, mom befriended a neighbor woman down the road who loved horses. We rode the bus with her kids. She talked mom into taking riding lessons from her, and shortly thereafter we added another horse to the stables named Colonel. Colonel was a beautiful white stallion, and my mother simply adored him. Unfortunately, he had a mind of his own, along with a serious fence-jumping problem. Between that and the fact that my dad could not control the horse to his liking, Colonel's days were obviously numbered. By 1960, so was my parents' marriage.

The divorce began with a legal separation initiated by my mother, and we lived in a rented house in the country about a mile from the farm. In those days, the vast majority of divorces ended with custody automatically going to the mother. However, my dad did not want my mother to get custody of us kids. Consequently, he was forced to show her incompetence to the judge to win custody rights. To accomplish this, he worked to mentally unsettle her. She was no match for him, and he pummeled her into extreme mental anxiety before, during, and after the divorce. She finally submitted to psychiatric care and electroshock treatments for depression, which, of course, went into the court record. This sufficiently convinced the legal authorities, and custody was eventually granted to dad and his third wife, the pretty little accountant, who was now to become our new stepmother. She also had one daughter who was added to our family number, but she was starting college at the time and was hardly ever at home.

During the time that my mother was being treated for depression, Colonel jumped what was to become his last fence. Dad and the hired hand, armed with a shot-gun and thirty-caliber rifle headed out into the north end of our property to find him. About two hours later, they brought him back dead on a hay wagon. The horse was promptly strung up by a chain harness in the middle of the barn-floor and butchered. Actually, it was an event attended by our whole family, and each of us participated in the process. I got my own knife and helped cut and hack with everyone else. For me, it was no different than going to town to get night crawlers for fishing; just another fun time with Dad. I didn't know it at the time, but the horse was butchered for food to supply our dog kennel. Dad later took the head and the four legs of the animal and put them in a fifty-gallon drum, placing them at the head of the barnyard. When my mother pulled in after her psychiatric discharge to collect her things that was the first sight she saw. It would be one of her last memories of the farm.

With the custody battle over, life seemed to return to normal, but things seemed markedly different. There was no more tension. My stepmother and dad seemed to get along fine and for me, all I remember was that life was filled with sunshine, blue skies, and a profound security in my family. I had a much different relationship with my stepmother than I had with my mother. She seemed to laugh more, and involved us more in domestic life, the doing of particular chores and such. I guess things were just more regimented, but we all actually liked it. I started kindergarten that year, and I loved going to school a half-day. Of course, it was probably good that the teacher only had me for a half-day. I was a real pistol. My dad took an interest in our education and attended the PTA meetings when they came up. My first PTA meeting results from my kindergarten teacher were interesting, at least to me.

We had a craft time each day that was supposed to allow for growth in our creative development. During clay modeling class one day I decided I would test my rock throwing skills by hurling a piece of clay at my teacher while she had her back turned to the class. My throw was extremely accurate, hitting her square in the back of her head. She quickly turned around while I pretended to be at work in my creative development. I happened to be at the kitchen table drawing pictures when Dad came home from the PTA meeting that night. He asked me about the incident. Whether I learned it there or had already learned it, you did not lie to my father. I got a spanking, and I assure you, it never crossed my mind to test my throwing skills in kindergarten class again.

CHAPTER THREE

What Day Is It?

MY LIFE, AS it seemed to me, was a perfect mosaic of
everything it was supposed to be. On the farm, my mind
was always filled with wonderful thoughts, and it
seemed like there were always more adventures than I
could ever take in. Every foot of ground dad owned was
a piece of my world, and that world, at least to me,
seemed indestructible and eternal. I knew the pasture,
the trees, and nearly every square inch of the riverbank.
We called it the crick. In the winter we skated on the
crick and built snow forts in our big back yard or down
in the pasture. In the summer we fished in the river,
swam in the pool, and barbequed in the back yard.
There were dogs, sheep, and horses to feed, a garden full
of good stuff to eat, and around us on every side was
farmland being cultivated which would eventually yield
corn, wheat, and soy beans. Life on the farm with my
doctor dad and new mom was seamless and blissful. I'm
sure there were some bad days, but I have little memory
of them. Not long after my stepmother and her daughter

joined our family, there was one unforgettable event.

Early one morning, my stepsister was driving her 1960 Volkswagen beetle to go to class at the university. A few miles from the house she pulled out in front of a car traveling too fast on an adjacent country road and was broadsided. The impact ejected her from the car. Unfortunately, the other driver's car was still operative, and the driver never stopped. The ambulance attendants found her nearly dead in the field several yards away from the accident scene. She had suffered massive brain, torso, and lower body injuries. All I remember is that my stepmother was at the hospital almost full-time. Dad also committed much time and effort to her healing and rehabilitation. During that six to ten week period, he hired a full-time nanny to take care of us at home. Her name was Mrs. C.

I could never forget this woman if I tried. She was a combination of Auntie Em and the Wicked Witch of the West. To make matters worse, we hated her cooking, especially her meatloaf. I honestly believe I've tasted better dog food.

One night while we were peacefully having supper with Mrs. C at the helm, we had a visitor. It was my stepsister's old boyfriend from the university. He was on the college diving team and was a tremendously strong and gifted athlete. He had not handled the reality of my stepsister's accident and subsequent injuries very well. This evening he was evidently depressed and taking barbiturates. Upon entering the kitchen, he began threatening Mrs. C and us kids for what had happened to his girlfriend, as if we were at fault. Fortunately for us, Mrs. C was no pushover, and a few minutes later he retreated and locked himself in the bathroom. He then passed out on the floor.

Mrs. C called a couple of local farmers and the Sheriff. Within minutes there were three or four burly farmers and two sheriff's deputies standing in our kitchen outside the bathroom door. This is no exaggeration. It took every one of them to get the young man out of our house that night. He took the bathroom sink and some of our plumbing with him. In reality, Mrs. C was just what the doctor ordered (quite literally), and after a few months, dad, my stepmother, and my step-sister were back home in the family circle. My stepsister's injuries were actually the catalyst for my dad to build our in ground pool. When he wanted to show it, dad had a tremendous capacity for compassion and love. Much of my stepsister's physical therapy took place in the pool with my dad, and as it would turn out, it was the swimming which made the most significant difference in putting her physical and emotional life back together.

There were some odd times during this home rehabilitation period that I can't forget. One night we were all around the table eating when my stepsister, still emotionally unwell, said she felt like screaming. Dad said, "Go ahead." And so, in the middle of a normal everyday family meal, my stepsister screamed bloody murder at the top of her lungs. I can still see the back of her throat. Despite these odd events, my security was never consciously affected. As long as dad was there, and our family was together, I felt a deep, almost indescribable security in our home. But as I would find out, it was not to last forever.

Initially, after the divorce and the settling of my stepmother, I thought that my real mother would never re-enter the picture. After all, I was happy and secure with my new "mom." But unknown to me, my real mother had petitioned the courts for monthly visiting privileges to her Cleveland home where she lived with her sister, Mary. Actually, none of us liked Mary, and when we were first told that we had to visit Mom in Cleveland, nobody wanted to go. It's hard to explain, but I actually didn't feel much love toward my mother either. I didn't understand it at the time, but it was probably because my mother, after learning of her pregnancy of me, wanted dad to let her have an abortion. Dad was against it. Lucky for me, but this was probably what was at the root of the lack of feeling and bond between us. Her love always seemed kind of empty and sterile. Years later, I would find that both my brother and sister had the same type of relationship with our mother.

On August 3, 1962, our mother and Mary picked my brother and me up on Friday night to take us to Cleveland for the weekend. My sister petitioned dad not to have to go, and so she stayed home. Saturday, we went to the Cleveland city zoo, and most of Sunday we visited with my mom's family and our cousins. On Monday morning Geoff and I were getting ready to take the car ride back home when our mother appeared in the doorway of the bathroom. She was there to tell us that our dad had died Sunday evening. I can't really describe the emotional trauma of the next few days, but death to any small child is indescribably surreal. All I knew is that a significant anchor in my life had drifted out to sea, and in some ways I felt like I had begun drifting too.

The date of my dad's death was August 5, 1962, the day that Marilyn Monroe also passed into eternity. He had played golf that morning with a few doctor friends at the country club in town and was home just after midday. About two that afternoon, he collapsed out in the yard with a massive heart attack. He seemed to understand the severity of the moment. In those days, there was little that was medically done for heart attack patients. Even aspirin was not understood to have therapeutic value at this time. Consequently, fatality rates were high. My stepmother told me that while he was laying there in the side-yard waiting on the ambulance, he did something very unusual. Slowly sitting up, he asked my stepmother, "What day is it?" She said, "Jeff, you have just had a heart attack. Why would you ask me that now?" He calmly replied, "I want to know the day of my death." After he said that, he laid back down on the grass and gave her the plans for his own funeral. He said that there would be no minister, no church, and no Bible reading. Rather, he wanted his jazz band to come and play at the memorial. He wanted to die as he had lived: like there was no tomorrow and no eternal consequences. And so it was. That Wednesday afternoon was the initial public viewing, and Thursday the family gathered for a final goodbye to the anchor of all of our lives. Dad's old jazz band was playing in the background. My final sight of him was when I asked a big man standing by the casket to lift me up so I could see him. I don't remember who it was, but he did as requested, and I kissed dad's face one last time.

CHAPTER FOUR

"Mother" and the Farm

I STARTED SECOND grade in September. The bus would pull right up to the front of our house on the little road between the house and the river. The bus ride was fun, but most of the time, I was thinking about getting back home and catching frogs or something. The connection I felt with everything called home was almost magical. It was the place I never wanted to be parted from for very long. And when I got back to it, it was like coming back to where I belonged.

Not long after school started, my stepmother told us at dinner one night that our mother had petitioned the court in light of my father's death, to regain custody of us kids. We wanted to know what that meant, and she told us that we might have to go live with her and our Aunt Mary in Cleveland. I don't remember much of the next few weeks, but I remember being in this little room inside the county court house being asked some questions by a woman. I don't know if I told her or told my brother to tell her, but the court report indicated that

I wished my mother was dead, so I didn't have to go live with her in Cleveland. My brother and sister testified in court that they didn't want to leave our stepmother or the farm either. Unfortunately, none of that mattered to the court, and our mother officially won custody rights.

Within days, our mother pulled into the barnyard in her black station wagon with Aunt Mary to take us somewhere none of us wanted to go. Now, for the second time in just a few months it seemed, life was about to take another wrong turn. But this one, we thought, was different. We had some say about it. At least we would be together, and maybe we could convince her that we didn't like it there and she would just send us back to our stepmother and the farm.

It's funny, but my memory of living with my mother and Aunt Mary in Cleveland is definitely sketchy. All I know is that we were determined to show our mother that we did not want to live with her. In fact, it was more than that. We wanted her to get the message that we hated her and thought she was a literal kook. Geoff and I shared an upstairs bedroom which quickly became our own battleground against mother. We would scribble messages to her on the walls with crayons. Such things as, "We hate you", and "We want to go home." At suppertime, we would start food fights and throw food at each other or at the walls. When we did the dishes, we would intentionally drop glasses and plates on the floor. Geoff would even build battery-powered robots with his erector set which he would just turn loose in the living room. Anything in the way of the crude machine would be broken, and it wasn't always to be blamed on the robot.

Finally, one day in November while on the way to school, my sister informed Geoff and me that we were heading to the bus station instead. Sure enough, my thirteen year-old sister proceeded to buy us tickets, and shortly after we were riding a Greyhound bus back across the state. Arriving around noon that day, we called our stepmother to come get us. She called the "social services office" to tell the caseworker what we had done, and in an hour or so, we were back on the farm. I'm not sure about the details of that day, but I know that our mother eventually conceded custody of us kids back to our stepmother. For us it was a moral victory. Perhaps, we thought, things could now just go back to what they were on the farm, and for the most part, they did.

One day the hired hand showed up after school with his coat pockets bulging. He called me over and asked me to hold out my hands, and when I did, he quickly placed two baby ducks into them. Of course I was completely elated and quickly began trying to figure out where I was going to keep them. We finally decided to use an old dog cage from my dad's dog show days to be their first home. It served the purpose quite well. I decided on the names Louie and Lieber. How I ever told them apart, I can't tell you. Every day, I would fill up an empty frozen orange juice tin with oats and feed both ducks out of the can. In a few months both had successfully grown up. After school, they would both come to me still looking for their can of oats. In a way, Bill's gesture of giving Louie and Lieber helped me to put distance between my

Dad's death and the saga of the custody battle. I was really home now, and I was confident that the thunder and lightening of life was over. I thought I had nothing but sunshine and blue skies ahead.

We continued to raise the sheep after dad died. It was not uncommon, when the lambs came in, to have a lamb or two that would be rejected by their mother. In such cases we would have to bottle-feed them until they could survive on their own. Later that first spring, I was given the job of feeding one such lamb every day after school. We had a small building by the kennel where we mixed feed. I would mix up three bottles of milk each day and go down to the pasture to a mass of scattered sheep. I would whistle, and out from the pack the abandoned lamb would start running to meet me at the gate, bellowing all the way. It would nurse those bottles one after another until he had milk foam all over his whole face. It was comical, and like everything else on the farm, it never occurred to me that there was any other way to live.

For instance, we had sulfur water in our well. It was so bad, we had to coal filter the water before it went into the cistern. Every so often, someone would have to go out and pour in a half-gallon of bleach to insure we were drinking "high quality" sulfur water. My brother and I were always outside doing something and when we got thirsty, we would usually just turn on the hydrant and drink straight from the spout. I don't know what you know about this kind of water, but not only does it have an odor, it also produces burps that smell like rotten eggs. Geoff and I thought this was entirely normal. In fact, when I was at school or at someone's house in town, I thought the city water was simply awful. Because I couldn't taste it and it didn't make me burp, I actually felt sorry for those poor city kids.

Of all the animals we had, I was most awed by the horses. However, there was one problem, they were too big for me to ride. Starting in the early spring of second grade, I began asking my stepmom for a pony. Quite honestly, somehow I knew I would never get a pony. After all, I was only in second grade, and I didn't know any other boy who had one. Anyway, by the time I got out of school in late May, I had forgotten all about it. My stepmom told us that in a few weeks we were going to get to go to a summer fun-camp for a week up in Michigan. This was a first for us. I thought my stepmom must still have been trying to help us get over losing dad.

Whatever the motive, going to a fun-camp with a bunch of other kids seemed like a great thing. And it was. For the first time in my brief mortal existence, I was not ready to go home after only a week at camp. I had made new friends, and had so much fun, I didn't want it to end. But coming back to the farm was the next best thing. The summer rolled into July and like every kid, the days seemed like they were endless adventures. We had our chores to do around the house, but when we were done, we could go swimming or fishing, play frisbee or football.

Not only that, but I kept asking for that pony.

At about ten o'clock one late July morning, Jerry, a family friend, turned into our driveway in his old Ford pick-up pulling a small trailer. He told me to go get my mother, and in a few minutes we were all standing in the barnyard watching him back the trailer up toward the barn door. My step-mom told me to watch him and help him if he needed it. I couldn't imagine what our neighbor was delivering that morning, but I could tell by the way my stepmother was acting; it was out of the ordinary.

As Jerry got out of the truck to come around to the back of the trailer, I still never thought that the delivery might be for me. He swung the door open, and there stood a beautiful Shetland pony. He was shiny black and had a white star right in the middle of his forehead. I must have looked overwhelmed, like a Christmas in July look. My stepmother began to laugh and told me it was mine as Jerry led him out of the trailer stall into the summer sun. Within seconds, my overwhelmed look turned to excitement, as I got a quick lesson on how to tie the saddle and properly place the bit in his mouth. Someone asked, "Bruce, what are you going to name him?" Knowing me, I probably gave them another dumb look, and my sister suggested, "Why not call him Bandit? He looks like one." Well, that settled it. Bandit was his name, and it stuck. Bandit and I spent a lot of time that summer getting to know the pasture and each other. As summer turned to fall and school started back, we spent less time together, but he was still the first one I fed when I helped Bill do the chores.

Actually, the fact that my stepmother gave me a pony does not really describe her personality entirely. She had another side of her, which was not so complimentary. For instance, she was a stickler about table manners.

One night while eating supper, I felt a sharp jab in my left elbow. For some reason I had forgotten to keep it off the table, and on that occasion, I paid for it with a jab from her fork. I looked over to see blood running down my arm and my stepmother's angry countenance for forgetting my manners again. If she had apologized at that moment for overreacting to such a minor infraction, I probably would have forgotten it. But all she did was get me a band-aid. On another occasion, not long after dad died, I had come downstairs one morning to go to the bathroom. The door was partly open so I stepped in thinking no one was there when all of a sudden my stepmother slammed the door shut on the end of my big toe. It turned the nail back and hurt terribly. Once again, there was little, if any sympathy shown, and no apology forthcoming. I wondered if she ever would have done that while dad was alive. It appeared that my stepmother could never do anything wrong enough to affect her own conscience. But like most youngsters, I was resilient, and I simply thought twice about walking through a bathroom door half-closed again.

I was now eight years-old and third grade marked a new level of learning. I was introduced to social studies, and we even got to see some science shows on television before recess. My brother was in sixth grade and still attended my elementary school. Geoff, for his size, was a very strong kid. He was well-liked by both the students and Mr. Sibes, his sixth grade teacher. Having a teacher who liked him helped him out of many sticky situations. For one thing, Geoff loved to fight out on the playground after lunch. It was usually the same boy every day. The kid was a bully, and Geoff had taken it upon himself to make sure he wasn't one of his victims. Actually, I think Mr. Sibes appreciated Geoff doing on the playground what he couldn't really fix in the classroom.

My sister Lee was a ninth grader at the Junior High School. Unlike me, her teachers would say great things about her on her report card, like "Lee shows great potential," and has "natural brilliance." I had the normal stuff like, "Bruce does well when he tries," or "Bruce needs better self-control."

One time, one of my city-slicker classmates brought a snapping turtle to class he had found in his back yard. They put it in a box, and they lined us up to walk by and see it for show and tell. Mrs. Podell, my teacher, strictly told the class not to put their hands into the box under any circumstances. Of course, I interpreted that command for the dumb city kids who had never seen a turtle before. Consequently, when it was my turn to walk by, I promptly showed my friends that snapping turtles were not to be feared by sticking my hand well into the box. The turtle obliged by latching on to the index finger on my left hand. Furthermore, in order to scare the dickens out the girls, I lifted my hand with the turtle on the end of my finger to establish my young manhood for all to see. Unfortunately, Mrs. Podell was not impressed. She immediately called my stepmother and I was forced to go home for the rest of the school day. It was not good. Most of the time however, I made it through the day, and we would all ride the bus home from school.

In February of 1964, the Beatles made their debut in America on the Ed Sullivan show. In no time, Beatlemania, as it was called, struck the nation and we were trading Beatle cards on the bus. For the Snavely kids, it was the third of a trinity of major events in our lives. Dad had died in 1962, President Kennedy was assassinated in 1963, and then appearing, as if to fill this great void, the Beatles arrived in 1964. Like many in the Boomer generation, this was the beginning of a new era. Little did we realize it then, but a new epoch was about to begin for us, too. It was one that my stepmother had already begun to hint at periodically in 1964. She was apparently having a hard time handling all the responsibilities of rural life, and it was possible that we might not be able to stay on the farm.

CHAPTER FIVE

Where Am I Going?

AS SPRING ROLLED around the next year in 1965, it had become clear that the farm and all the property were going to have to be sold. My stepmom had arthritis in both hands and complained that since there were several things that required her attention on the farm, moving had become inevitable for our family. I remember the real estate lady that came to the house. She was always well dressed and drove a big Cadillac. We would all get in and go driving around looking at houses on the weekends. By the time school got out, we had looked at several houses, even some well out of town.

The one house that we all seemed to like was this huge Victorian mansion house in Waterville, Ohio. It's now registered with the local historical Society, but in 1965, it was just another available house on Canal Street, overlooking the Anthony Wayne Trail. It was flanked by woods on one side and was a few hundred yards from our nearest neighbor. It had a large garage in the back with an apartment above it for rent. The house had a library room, a long, wide staircase, and a secret back staircase off the upstairs sewing room, which led to a small bar back downstairs just off the living room. It wasn't anything like the farm, but for some reason, it seemed like it was going to be a real fun place to live. Out behind the main property was an old farm silo, and the rear acreage led back to railroad tracks which meandered southwest through town.

It was about the middle of July when the sale was final on our new house. We never did meet the new buyers of the farm. Everything seemed to be focused on the new house in Waterville. I don't remember any ceremonious goodbyes or tearful moments with the animals. In fact, over the spring and early summer, most everything had been slowly pared down. The sheep had been sold, the kennel dogs were all sold off, and we had plenty of horse people around the farm that showed interest in the three or four horses we had left.

Even Bandit had to be sold, because there was no barn or horse facility at the new house.

I think I handled it ok, because Bandit was young, and like me, I figured he was just as excited about what the future held as I was. The one thing I think I missed the most was the river. For my brother and me, it had always been at the center of everything else we did. If we weren't wading, fishing, or catching frogs and turtles in the summer, we were skating and playing hockey on it in the winter months. You could skate in either direction for a mile or so and never get lost. All you had to do was just turn around and skate, and you would eventually make it all the way home.

The morning we left the farm, the nice real-estate lady picked us up in her big Cadillac to deliver us to our spacious, new house. Not long after we got there, the Mayflower moving van arrived and our new life officially got started. August seemed to fly by and before I knew it, school was already starting at my new school. I was beginning my fourth grade year. Geoff was in his first year of junior high school; Lee was in her sophomore year of high school, and we all three rode the bus in different directions each morning.

I must say, fourth grade was an awesome year for me. By late fall, the family routine was seemingly back in order. My stepmother was working for my dad's former partner in the pathology Laboratory in Bowling Green, and home life seemed pretty normal to me. I had made a lot of new friends, and I loved riding my bike up and down my new street. I even had a classmate who lived a few doors down, and they had a barn on the back of their property with a few horses, not to mention a go-cart. But, that fall in my new house on Canal Street, my biggest memory was Halloween. It was the first time I had gotten to walk from house to house trick or treating. My brother and sister dressed me up, and I joined up with a few neighbor friends on Friday night. In about an hour or so, I was dragging home a brown paper bag almost full of every kind of candy imaginable. I thought this was like an early Christmas. I wasn't allowed to eat any before I went to bed, but Saturday morning, I poured it all out on my bed to count it. It was truly the haul of the century. I couldn't imagine life getting much better than this.

By early spring of 1966, fourth grade was moving well along and I heard that baseball tryouts were going to be held in a couple of weeks in our local park. I signed up at school and asked my stepmother if I could join. She gave permission, and a few weeks later, I was the official left fielder for our local peewee team. At the team meeting for our first game, Coach Sweeney told us to be there no later than 6:30. Somehow, I thought he said 8:30, and by the time I arrived everybody was just leaving the field. I was completely deflated and angry with myself for not listening better to the coach. Fortunately for me, that never happened again, but it was a hard lesson to forget.

As a boy, baseball was definitely my sport. I had terrific hand-eye coordination at the plate, so there was nothing I couldn't hit. My batting average hovered between 500 and a 1000 all year. In the field, I thought that you weren't supposed to ever have anything go over your head, and so nothing did. I was fast and agile for my age, and like my dad once said, I was healthy and aggressive.

I also had a great confidence builder in my fourth-grade baseball career. My stepmom had rented out our garage apartment to a player for the Toledo Mud Hens, the Detroit Tiger's farm club. He was an outfielder like me, so occasionally on his days off, he would shag balls with me and help me work on my hitting. I don't remember his name, but one time he got me tickets to one of his games. I don't think I ever thought how lucky I was to have a semi-pro baseball player living right in my back yard. My coach was always praising me, and my confidence level that spring and summer was off the charts. The coach's son Jake and I were best friends. He was the only kid in the world that I would ever split a jawbreaker with—even after he had already chewed it.

Jake seemed to understand that I didn't have a dad at the games like the other kids, so he didn't appear to mind his dad praising me for playing well. I didn't really feel sorry for myself for not having a dad anymore. I must have thought that all the kids were just like me, and that all the folks in the stands were simply baseball enthusiasts from around the park, not moms and dads of players. I never actually thought of it unless someone asked me where my dad was, and I would just tell them he had died. You never think people know anything about you and your family when you're a kid, but, of course, people ask questions, and certainly they must have wondered about me. Sometimes my stepmother would come to my games, but not often. Consequently, I usually didn't arrive at the park in a family car like most kids.

Our house sat about 500 yards from a set of railroad tracks on the back of our property. On practice days and game nights, I would take a path through the weeds to walk the tracks down to the city park where we played. After the game, I would walk the tracks home. For me, this seemed entirely normal, and I was used to it.

Actually, all through that spring of 1966, things were beginning to change around our house. Our stepmother was becoming noticeably different toward us and seemed to be estranged and busy. Of course, my sister was a full-fledged teenager, and my brother and I weren't exactly angels, but there was something going on, which I don't think any of us quite understood at the time. Mom seemed to be drinking a lot, and home life was a little erratic.

One day my sister, Lee even went so far as to call our real mother in Cleveland to tell her about how our stepmother was acting. This seemed kind of odd to me because we had never wanted to have her back in our lives after dad had died. It seemed like all of us kids were a little on edge about the way our stepmother was treating us, and I think at that point, we were probably hoping that somehow there would be someone who could intervene for us and make our situation better. Looking back, it was really more an act of desperation than a calculated move. There was really no one else in our lives to either offer help or give it, and reaching out to our birth mother, who for all intents and purposes had legally and emotionally signed off on us, was indeed strange. For me, it was probably not as unsettling as it was for my brother and sister. Being older and more mature, they knew that something wasn't right, but they were at a loss for knowing what it was, or what to do about it.

But, as winter melted into spring that year, there were other things that helped maintain some normality. For one, my stepsister had married and was expecting sometime in late May or June, and step mom had planned a spring baby shower for her. About the beginning of April, my stepsister's new husband came up to Waterville on a Friday night to have a boy's night out with Geoff and me during the shower. We all went out to a drive-in movie to see "The Ghost and Mr. Chicken" starring Don Knots. We had never spent much time with him and going out was a lot of fun.

We have a way of only remembering things we want to, and as I recall, the drive-in that night was more than just a movie—it was an event! Not only did it help Geoff and me forget about stuff at home, but this was one of the few men we had spent quality time with since we had moved off the farm. Our dad's loss was more apparent than any of us realized at the time.

The one thing that eclipsed anything negative in life that spring was baseball. It was truly the highlight of my life. I couldn't wait to play, and the routine was great. I would just walk out my backdoor, walk through my backyard down a walking path to the railroad tracks behind our house, turn left and walk the tracks about a quarter of a mile to the city park baseball diamond. Whether it was practice, a game, or the orange snow cone on my walk back home, I loved the sense of adventure from the time I left the house.

But by mid-June, the peewee season was over, school was out, and summer had arrived. Geoff and I would get up after our stepmother left for work, have some cereal and usually head outdoors. Being farm kids and adventurous, I think we would have lived outdoors if our stepmother would have let us. There was always something to do. If it were raining, we would do our inside jobs and listen to Beatle records or AM radio. Since my sister was the reigning teenager in the house, she picked the records and determined how loud the volume was set. I think it was about this time that I began to tell time by what songs were playing on the radio.

I remember three songs that I heard a lot on CKLW the summer of '66: *Louie, Louie* by the Kingsmen, *Wild Thing* by the Trogs, and *Nowhere Man* by the Beatles. I always got mad at my brother and sister because they would never tell me what the lyrics to *Louie Louie* were actually saying. They, like the rest of American teens at the time, were convinced that there were "dirty" sexual lyrics imbedded in the song, and that they knew them, but wouldn't tell me. I guess it's good they never did, because it was all just a big hoax anyway, simply another innocuous love song of the sixties.

The summer of '66 in Waterville, Ohio, rolled on through July. I wasn't even thinking about starting fifth grade. If summer is a time of transition, I was definitely not moving forward. It was more like sideways. I was addicted to green grass, blue skies, puffy clouds, and staying up a little later than usual. But in the midst of my bright summer skies, something dark and ominous was approaching, and unfortunately, there were no warning signs.

About the last week of July, I got up one morning, went to the bathroom, and then had just started to head downstairs for cereal when I saw the dining room table filled with my clothes. I saw my stepmother standing there, and it reminded me of the day she was packing our stuff for fun-camp. I asked, "Mom, are we going to camp?" She hesitated, and then simply said, "No Bruce, you're leaving this morning." I slowly walked down the stairs, and noticed that she had been crying, and that meant this was a very weird morning, because I had never seen her cry about anything.

I immediately began to wonder what had happened. Why was she doing this? Had I done something wrong? Was it because she had caught me smoking one of her cigarettes out in the old silo one day? But I had gotten punished for that, I thought. Certainly, this couldn't be for that. I had done all my chores. I hadn't lied or anything. I was afraid to ask what I had done to deserve this, I don't know why. Then my brother came down and got the same news. It's funny, in a way, I was relieved that Geoff was going with me, but neither of us had any idea what was actually happening to us. Then Lee came down into all this confusion, and it appeared as if Lee was going to get to stay, because my stepmother had said that the welfare department lady was coming only to pick Geoff and me up at eleven o'clock that morning. We were going to be taken to a group home, and then be placed in a foster home.

What's a foster home? I thought.

Geoff and I wandered outside and tried to comprehend what was going on. We decided to play catch with the football and try to be normal. Maybe, then all this stuff would go away. But for the next few hours, nothing was normal, and it wouldn't go away. Even the most familiar things like trees and birds and wind and sky seemed different, almost threatening. I hadn't seen it coming, but my young life was destined to change that morning.

My familiar was eerily becoming unfamiliar. My courage was being introduced to fear, and my rock-solid world was being invaded by insecurity. I was no longer invincible, and deep inside I knew it, but what made it worse was the fact that neither of us knew where we were going. What we did know was that some stranger from the welfare department was coming in a few hours to take us away from everything that mattered.

CHAPTER SIX

Where's Home?

IT WAS WELL past eleven, when the car we feared was coming finally pulled into our tree-lined driveway. In the meantime, Lee had gotten in an argument with our stepmother about the phone call she had made the previous week to our real mother in Cleveland. I don't know why we called her, we didn't even love her. I guess we just needed to make ourselves feel better about the insecurity we were getting from our stepmom. I really don't think any of us wanted to go live with her, but at that point, things seemed kind of unpredictable. By the time the argument was over, Lee too, was packing a bag and coming along with Geoff and me.

In less than an hour the welfare lady, Mrs. Finch, had us packed into the station wagon, and we were heading to a house in Bowling Green, a sort of group home for yet to be placed orphans. It had a temporary feel to it, and sure enough I was picked up three days later by my assigned caseworker and carted off to my first full-time foster home. I remember my caseworker's name was

Judy. She reminded me a little of my step-mother's daughter. I was introduced to her in the group home kitchen, and Mrs. Finch told me to take my things to her car. Judy was nice, but detached, and she really didn't talk to me about anything, at least not anything that I wanted to talk about. I wanted answers to my questions like; "Why are you taking me away from my brother and sister?" "Why can't we stay together?" Or the big question, "What did I do to make my stepmother do this to me?" Oh, and then there was the question, "When do I get to see my brother and sister again?" We talked about none of that. It was just a very empty car ride, with all of my unasked questions and no answers, the drone of her Volkswagen beetle taking me someplace I didn't know, and the ache of my ten year-old broken spirit.

To say that life had changed in three days didn't come near to what I was feeling. Somehow I knew inside that it was never going to be the same again. My secure, happy life as I had once known it was over, and the future seemed ominous and frightening. All of sudden I didn't know where home was anymore.

After about an hour of driving, we pulled into the driveway of a nice, neat little ranch style house and stopped. Judy informed me that this was my new family, and they wanted me to come live with them. I really didn't want any part of it. She opened her door to get out and told me to do the same. We got out and slowly walked up to the door just inside the carport. A friendly woman appeared at the door and stepped outside to greet us. She had already met Judy previously, so she looked at me and introduced herself. "Hi Bruce, I'm

Nora, and we are so happy that you are here to live with us," and just behind the door stood her two kids, a boy and a girl. Looking around she said, "This is Tommy and Jenna. Come out and say hi to Bruce." I wanted to be nice and normal but it seemed impossible to control my feelings. I didn't ask for this family. I didn't even like the way they looked. I tried to be charming and said hi. But I just wanted to go home.

It all seemed crazy.

I wish someone had just sat me down and told me what was going on, because nothing seemed to make sense at all. I was hoping they had heard of my family, knew my stepmother or something, and we could get all this straightened out, and they could take me home in a few days. No such luck. They didn't know of me or my family, and they didn't know anything about what was going on with me. Everything was just kind of bundled up inside of me and left there. It was like I had been thrown into an ocean and just told to swim, and I felt that at any minute I could drown. Judy quickly got my things out of the car, and a few minutes later, my first lifeline to reality was gone again. I watched the red beetle back out of the driveway and drive away, and for the first time in my life, I think I was beginning to understand what it must be like to be alone.

Nora asked me if I would like to see my bedroom, so I walked inside. Tommy and Jenna were looking at me while their mother was telling me about my room and where to put my stuff. I had to share the room with Tommy. He wasn't much like me at all, so I wasn't looking forward to it. I spent the afternoon watching TV and as Nora was fixing supper, her husband came home from work. He came into the TV room and introduced himself. "Hi Bruce, I'm Duane. Welcome to our home. Are you hungry? Supper is about ready, so why don't you and Tommy wash your hands and come to the table."

In a few minutes Duane, Nora, Tommy, Jenna, and I were gathered around the table in the kitchen ready to eat. Duane said a blessing over the food, and we began to pass the food. As I would find out, the Rinde family was a lot more religious than I had been used to. We went to church every Sunday morning and once during the week too. Their church taught that you had to be baptized to be a Christian, so every time I went to church, I was invited to come forward for baptism. For some reason, I never did it.

After church, and sometimes after supper, Duane would throw the football with me. He could lay an underhanded pass on target at a long distance. So I would run across the biggest part of their yard and catch his underhanded long bombs just before reaching the high weeds in the adjacent field. It was one of the few things I did that made me feel good. I guess it reminded me of my brother and home. Most of the time however, I thought about nothing but how much I wanted to get my family back. I didn't have much in common with Tommy. He was a year younger than I was.

I was a tough kid who had grown up on the farm. He was a pasty little kid who seemed weird to me. For one thing, when I got there, he had just had a hernia operation, and the doctor had sewed his scrotum to his leg to prohibit movement. I didn't understand it fully at the time, and it just seemed like he was a dumb kid who couldn't walk right. To make things worse, he would put himself to sleep at night by rocking in his bed. He would lie on his stomach and pull his knees up to his chest and then lay down flat again. It would take fifty to a hundred repetitions before he would finally put himself to sleep. Sometimes I would drift off first, other times I would have to listen to every repetition.

Not long after I arrived at the Rindes, school started. Being at a brand-new school was nearly as hard as leaving home. I knew no one, and of course nobody knew me either. I was surprised on about the third day when I was going down the hall to lunch, I saw my Little League Coach. I said, "Hi Coach Sweeney!" He looked really glad to see me and said, "Hey, Bruce" with sort of a surprised look on his face. Time wouldn't permit any conversation, and unfortunately, that was the first and only time I ever saw my old coach. He didn't know what my stepmother had done, and I always wondered if he would have been as interested in me as an orphan as much as he was a baseball player. I thought of Jake and how much I missed the baseball scene at home.

It wasn't long before my behavior began to spiral out of control at the Rinde's house. Duane and Nora used to pick up this woman for the mid-week service at church who smoked. After about three weeks or so of picking her up, I stole a pack of her cigarettes while at her house one night after church. After school the next day, I went out in the woods behind the house and smoked some. I don't know why, but I think it made me feel like I was in control. But control was not my only motivation.

I was also angry inside.

I wanted someone to listen to me, to know what I was feeling, and it just wasn't happening. About the second week in October I was getting ready to go to school. I was feeling unusually agitated about my situation that day. While in the living room waiting for the bus, I looked at Mrs. Rinde's metronome on her electric organ in the corner. I had heard her say that she had saved Green Stamps for several years in order to have enough to get this ornate timing instrument. It was a brass work in a beautiful mahogany case, and I knew she really liked it. I picked it up, took the top off it, and deliberately bent the timing piece until it broke off. I placed it back inside, put the top back on, and went out and caught the bus.

I actually forgot about it until I got home from school that day. While getting off the bus, I noticed my caseworker Judy was at the house, and all my stuff was again packed in her Volkswagen. I instinctively realized that my bad behavior had gotten some attention, unfortunately it wasn't positive. Less than twenty minutes later, I was leaving the Rinde's house and heading off to my third foster home in less than three months.

As we backed out of the Rinde's driveway, I had a silent yet certain sense of accomplishment well up inside me. I had actually precipitated an event in my own life. I had in a very small measure, gotten some control of my life. It wasn't pretty, but I knew that what I had done to Nora's metronome had earned me a ticket out of there, and I secretly hoped it might be a step towards home. Unfortunately, it wasn't long before I realized I wasn't going home.

We drove about forty-five minutes to another part of the county I had never been in before. Just off a secondary road I had seen maybe once, we meandered down a few country roads and slowly pulled into a long stone driveway of a large farmhouse set back from the road. As we pulled up to the side of the house I could see another little house in back that was hidden from view. Judy slowly brought the car to a stop, turned off the motor, turned and said, "Let's go in and meet your new family." For some reason, this one felt different to me. It might have been that it was the end of the day, I was hungry, and there were some really good smells coming out the back door. It might have been that it was a farm, and I felt comfortable in a strange place for the first time since I had left home. Whatever it was, this place seemed more inviting than the Rindes.

Judy stepped ahead of me and started up the back steps to knock on the door. Before we knocked a woman older than I expected came out the door to greet us. She said hi to Judy and then looked right into my eyes and said hi to me. She seemed happy to see us, and I immediately felt good in her presence. She said, "Hi Bruce, I'm Iona, come on in the kitchen." There was a little breezeway where all the work coats and shoes were, and then there was a step up into the kitchen. She was just beginning to get supper ready, and said her farmer husband Leroy would be in from the field in about a half hour. My caseworker and Iona talked for a few minutes while I was making friends with Toby the dog. He was just a brown mutt, but like Mrs. Warner, he seemed to like me. Judy interrupted and asked if I would bring my things in from the car and put them on the back porch. Mrs. Warner said her son Tom would be home from basketball practice in a few minutes and would help me carry them up to my room. After I brought my stuff in she showed me my room upstairs. I had my own room right across the hall from Tom. Mrs. Warner said Tom was a freshman in high school that year and was playing on the freshman team. I was in fifth grade, so Tom was four years older than me, but I still thought it was cool that I would have someone like a brother living across the hall. I secretly hoped that he was the kind of guy that liked playing catch and stuff.

After we came downstairs, Judy said it was time to be headed back to Bowling Green to finish her day. She seemed to sense that I appeared to be happy for the moment. She shook Mrs. Warner's hand and then turned and patted me on the shoulder. I'm sure she hoped this one would last longer than a month, and for some reason I thought it probably would. In a few minutes she was backing down the long driveway, and I was left alone in the kitchen with Mrs. Warner. She asked me if I was excited about seeing my new school in the morning. For a moment I was shocked to remember that I was going to have to make friends all over again at a new school, but Mrs. Warner seemed to sense my unease. She said she knew everybody in town, and I was going to love my teacher and my new classmates. I asked her why she knew so many people, and she said, "I work at the bank right in town. Almost everybody in town comes in the bank at least once a week. A lot of them already know you are coming." For some reason, that made me feel better. In fact, I was actually looking forward to going to school the next day—but just then I realized that the Rindes had not just decided today that I would be leaving.

A few minutes later the screen door slammed and her son Tom bounded into the kitchen from basketball practice. He kissed his mom, and she quickly introduced me. "Tom, this is Bruce. He just got here about a half-hour ago. I showed him his room, but he needs some help taking his things up, would you mind helping him?" In a flash, Tom and I had my stuff in my new room. He took the time to show me where to put some stuff away, and then he showed me his room across the hall. He was a teenager now, and I could tell he was going to be a lot of fun to be around. He had a record player in his room, and I could see that he liked the Beach Boys. He had two of their albums sitting in the record stand. He asked me what sports I liked to play. I told him I liked baseball and football mostly. He told me that they had a basketball rim in the barn and if I wanted we could shoot some after supper. All of sudden, Mrs. Warner called up the stairs that supper was ready. We were supposed to wash our hands. I also heard a man's voice in the kitchen and when I stepped into the kitchen, I met Mr. Warner. He was leaning over in the chair taking off his work boots and looked up as I came in. He was a short, sort of stocky man with a weathered face. I looked at him, and he reached out his hand and shook mine. He was without doubt, one of the kindest men I think I had ever met. I don't think Leroy Warner had a mean bone in his whole body. I liked him from the start, and I think he liked me too. We all sat down and Mr. Warner prayed a blessing over the food, just like at the Rinde's.

After supper, true to his word, Tom told his mom we were going out to the barn to shoot some baskets. Iona said that we could have some warm chocolate-chip cookies and milk when we came in later. In a few minutes Tom introduced me to the barn. It was a lot like the one I grew up around, except there were places on the sides of the barn, inside the fence where you could pull tractors in out of the weather. The barn floor was pretty even and on the back wall, Tom and his dad had installed a basketball hoop. We played for about an hour and it was already dusk when we went back out into the yard, and shut the barn door for the night. I listened to the crickets chirping as we walked over the barnyard to the house. That was a familiar sound. As I walked in the back screen-door I could see there was a light on at the little house out back that I noticed when we had driven in that afternoon. There was a flicker of a television and an older couple sitting down in the front room. I said, "Who is that in there?" Tom said, "That's my Grandma and Grandpa. They live here on the property too."

We went in and Tom poured both of us a glass of milk and got the Tupperware container of his mom's fresh cookies off the counter, and we both sat down at the table. I think for the first time since I had left home that unforgettable summer morning, I was beginning to feel an awkward sense of normalcy. It wasn't home, and this was not my family, but somehow I was getting a glimmer of hope back in my soul. I just hoped someone wouldn't come along and take it away. I was aware now that this was a real possibility in life.

I started in my new school the next day and seemed to make some friends quickly. I was outgoing and easy to talk to, so I readily attracted new friends. Life settled down into a routine that fall. School was going along just fine, and home life was more than tolerable on the farm. On Friday nights, we would sometimes go out to Tom's high school football games, but most Friday nights, my buddies and I would meet at the local roller skating rink. On Saturdays, Tom I would race his new go-cart up and down the long driveway and into the barn yard.

The one thing I liked about Tom was the fact that even though I wasn't his real brother, he wasn't selfish with his stuff. One day his dad took him to Sears, and he bought a new pellet gun. It was a pump pellet gun, but with enough pumps, a pellet could have almost the hitting power of a .22 caliber rifle. We always pumped it up to the max. When Tom got used to his new gun, he gave me his old BB gun. Usually when I got home from school, I would get my BB gun and go "hunting." Toby, our outside dog, and I would go out into the apple orchard and shoot sparrows for target practice. You wouldn't do that today and get away with it, but back in the 60's, especially if you were in the country, you did pretty much what you wanted. Sparrows were so plentiful; you couldn't count them if you tried. Toby usually ate the birds after I'd shoot them. One day I counted twenty-two sparrows, and Toby ate every last one of them.

Just after Christmas, we started going to Tom's high school basketball games on Friday nights. I was always amazed at the huge crowds in the high school gym on game nights. In farm country, players had family and friends to support them at the game, so the games were really exciting to watch. When the team was playing out of town, I would be skating at the rink. As spring rolled around that year, there were some signs put up at school that advertised Little League baseball. I was so excited to play my second year of Little League. I played left field again and couldn't wait for every practice and every game. When school got out in May, we continued playing into June. The Warners enjoyed coming to my games and seeing me play. Sometimes Leroy would miss if he was in the field, but if he could make it, he would.

One night after one of my games, Leroy and Iona told me they had something very important to talk to me about. They acted like it was something out of the ordinary. As we sat down in the kitchen, they told me that the Welfare Department had called them earlier in the week and told them about a prospect in which they thought I might be interested. It was a private school for boys in Hershey, Pennsylvania. As they told me about it, it seemed like they were unusually excited about what this could mean for me. I didn't feel like they wanted me to go, but I could tell that they thought this was an extraordinary prospect. As I listened to their description of the school, it sounded almost too good to be true. The school had ultra-modern homes, schools, athletic facilities, and academic opportunities unavailable anywhere else in the world. For some strange reason, it seemed like this was almost providential. Maybe, I thought that my luck had changed, and everything was going to turn around. The Warners said that if I wanted to go see it, that the welfare department would fly both Geoff and me to Hershey that weekend for a tour of the school.

Two days later, on a Friday morning, the social worker, Judy, Geoff, and I boarded a TWA flight to Harrisburg, Pennsylvania. We landed in a few hours and drove directly to Hershey to see the school. I don't remember a whole lot about the tour that afternoon. All I recall is that the campus was huge in terms of geographical size. It was located on hundreds of acres of land outside of Hershey, the "chocolate" town, named after Milton Snavely Hershey. Hershey had a great desire to help orphaned children and decided that he and his wife Catherine would use some of their chocolate profits to build a school for boys who had lost one or both parents. Since I had lost my dad, and was a ward of the state, I had a ticket in the door. In terms of academics and amenities, it was, and still is today, second to none. At that time, it seemed to me as if it was going to be like a huge, year-around summer camp. I was definitely all in. Geoff wasn't quite as exuberant about it, but he thought anything would be an improvement on his latest foster home. So, a couple of weeks later in July, 1967, Geoff and I were off to the Milton Hershey School in Chocolate Town, USA.

Saying goodbye to the Warners was a mixture of excitement and doubt, but I think I was truly excited about the move. It wasn't but just a few hours after they delivered me to my house unit, that I realized this was not summer camp. The school had three divisions:

Junior, Intermediate, and Senior. The Intermediate division housed sixth-grade to eighth-grade boys. This division had eight or so clusters of homes, with eight to ten homes in each cluster. Each cluster or division had a name. I was in the National cluster and was placed in the Lincoln home. Each of these ultra-modern homes had seven bedrooms and could sleep up to fifteen boys. The National cluster was known for being a very strict no-nonsense division. My house-parents were young parents who had one child. All house-parents lived in an apartment within the house but totally independent of the living quarters of the boys.

During the school year, the day started for us boys at five-thirty in the morning with the snap of a light switch that turned on every bedroom light simultaneously. The sound that surge of electricity created was enough to make you sit up and be wide-awake almost instantly. After the lights went on, we had fifteen minutes to make our beds, get dressed, and begin our first job before breakfast. The job might be anything from cleaning the back stairwell to the basement or vacuuming the boys' bedrooms. When your job was finished, you called for one of the older boys whose job was to inspect the work of the younger ones. Normally, if any dirt or dust could be produced on a white rag, you were forced to do the job over again. If this happened more than once on any given day, you might have to go to your second job and miss your breakfast. After breakfast you would go do your second job and then go get ready for school. Before leaving the house in our unit, boys lined up at the front door with their books in their right arms while reaching into their back left pocket to prove they had both a comb and hankie. If you didn't have it, you went back upstairs and got them. The comb and hankie habit stayed with me until I was forty.

One day I caught myself looking for my comb when I realized that I never needed to comb my hair anyway, and my wife hated my hankies. That was the end of that habit. Well, after we passed personal inspection, we were hurried out the door. Fifteen boys walked down the long drive of our cluster out to the main road, which, after a brief hike of a quarter mile, brought you to front door of Catherine Hall.

Catherine Hall was a beautiful three-level building at the time, which housed all of the classes for the entire division. It was named after Hershey's wife. On the far end of the complex was a furnished Gymnasium that attached to a full-sized Olympic pool and diving facility. To the rear of the Gymnasium was an ice hockey arena. For the two years I was at the school I played hockey, swam on the swim team, competed in gymnastics, and played in the marching band. On top of that, the academics were stellar. I couldn't have asked for greater opportunities. After my second year of playing hockey we had a hockey banquet and the school invited the Hershey Bears, an American League Hockey Team. We stayed close to the parking lot that night, and when the players exited their cars the first kid to ask for their stick got a good souvenir. Finally it was my chance, and I got the stick of one of the Bear's defensemen, Barry Ashbee. Barry was a big strong guy whose trademark was a stick with its blade slightly cut off on the end. He told us that it made his shot a little harder. Barry went on to play with the Philadelphia Flyers and won a Stanley Cup in the 1973-74 season. His career ended in 1974 when he was hit directly in the eye with a puck. In April 1977, he received the devastating news that he was dying of Leukemia. He died one month later. But that night, Barry skated with us like a schoolboy and really seemed to enjoy being with us kids.

Unfortunately though, even with all the athletic stuff, an ultra-modern home, sterling academics, and the smell of chocolate in the air almost every day, I hated being in the school. You have to understand, I wanted one thing, and that was to get my family back. Everything else, no matter how great, seemed like it was just in the way. You could have come up and offered me a million dollars, and I don't think I would have taken it, especially if you had my brother, sister, and yes, even my stepmother in the other hand. Every day I got up, I hoped it was the last one without my family.

We did have visitation privileges every month, but that really didn't matter for me. For the two years I was at MHS, I had only one person come to see me, and it wasn't my stepmother, real mother, aunt or uncle, or any other immediate family member. It was my half-sister Joan. Joannie, as we called her, was my Dad's daughter with his first wife. We had the same dad but different mothers. For some reason, she never forgot about me from the farm. Years after dad had divorced Betsy, Joannie came out to the farm on several occasions to visit. I don't know how she heard about Geoff and me being in Hershey, but she did, and she came to visit us one Saturday. It was nice at the time, but it was hardly satisfying to an eleven year-old kid wanting his own family back. I guess it was hard for me to have feelings for someone I only knew in connection with a few visits to the family farm when I was a toddler. Other than Joannie's one visit, I spent my Saturday afternoons wondering if someone would ever come take me out for the day. I had realized by this time that I was on my own now. My family and my memories of them were slowly beginning to fade into the past, and I could do little about it.

To my surprise, during my seventh grade year, my history teacher, Mr. Halbaker asked me after class one day if I would like to come visit his house on the following Saturday. He had gotten permission to take me out for visitation, and the next weekend he picked me up and took me to his house with a bunch of other boys. I realized then that I wasn't the only one who didn't have regular visitation. There were three or four of us there that day. We ate, played games, watched TV, and messed around with the player piano. There was something else that visit made me realize. I didn't have any family who cared enough about me to come see me. Other than Joannie, an anonymous teacher had shown more interest in me than anyone else in my whole world.

At the end of my first year at MHS, Geoff got lucky and was permanently taken out of the school. My aunt and uncle from Cleveland took him. It never crossed my mind why they didn't take me too but as a result, my seventh grade year was the loneliest I'd experienced to date. Geoff had been in another division, but I knew he was in the same school. I wondered constantly if I was going to have to spend the rest of my growing up at the boys' school without any family and without visitors. At the end of that school year Geoff asked my aunt and uncle if I could spend my month's summer vacation in Cleveland with them. Uncle Jim and Aunt Marcia lived on a little lake outside of Chagrin Falls, a quaint little town just east of the city. It was so much fun to spend time with Geoff and to actually be with people I was related to for a change. During the whole month of July, Geoff and I went swimming in the lake nearly every day, and I got to hang out with him and his friends.

One night, not long before I had to go back to school, some of Geoff's friends invited us over for a swim party. It was a wealthy family whose boys were the same age as Geoff and me. They had a huge house and an in ground pool. We swam and ate hot dogs well into that summer night. On the way home, Geoff told me they had asked about me and why we didn't live together. He told them our story and about the boy's school and how I was not happy there. He told them that I wanted to be near him, but Uncle Jim didn't have the room to take me because they already had three kids of their own plus Geoff. Mr. Williams told Geoff that they would look into the possibility of taking me out of the school.

A few nights later around sunset Geoff took me on his motorcycle around the backside of the lake behind our uncle's house. It was my last day of summer vacation, and I would be riding a bus back to Hershey the next morning. He stopped and for a few minutes we both stared across the lake while the sun went down. Neither of us said anything, but we both were thinking the same thing about what Mr. Williams had told Geoff at the pool party. After a few minutes, Geoff finally broke the silence: "We're going to get you out of there Bruce, don't worry." For the first time in a long time, I felt a surge of hope come up inside me the size of Mount Everest. I knew that Geoff would have never said that if the Williams were not serious about taking me out of the school. The hardest thing now was the uncertain wait. When would it happen? School would be starting back in just over a month, and I did not want to go back for another year by myself, especially after a summer vacation like that. But as scheduled, the next day, Uncle Jim and Geoff put my bag in the VW and we headed to Cleveland to the bus station.

It was a long, dismal trip back to Hershey. I didn't know my future, and the hope of what Geoff had said to me was all I had. When I got back to MHS, I began to fear the possibility that my hope was just a great big empty dream. Everything was back to normal, and there was only a little more than a month before school started back. Worse yet, I couldn't talk with anybody about my secret hope. Nobody would have listened anyway, and I didn't want anyone to mess it up, especially my house parents. I feared that if I said anything, it might get back to them, and they would do something to spoil the plan. Consequently, I suffered along in silence hoping that any day a phone call would change my life. Two weeks later, that phone call hadn't come, so I started making plans on running away. I didn't want to spend another year in Hershey. Nothing else mattered to me. I just wanted to get out. If I wasn't in Chagrin Falls before school started back, I'd be gone.

About the middle of August, nearly all of us boys were playing baseball up at the ball field about three in the afternoon. Out of nowhere, one of the kids came running up from the unit calling my name. I looked down and saw a big brown Buick station wagon sitting in the driveway. I remembered it from Chagrin that night after swimming at the William's. For a minute, I couldn't believe my eyes. I had no idea they were coming. Nobody had told me I was getting out. Almost numb, I ran down from the ball field for what I knew would be the last time. My housemother called me over to see the Williams. I must have looked like a kid on Christmas morning. They reminded me of their kid's names, and then asked me if I was ready to go home with them. Before I could say anything, my housemother got my attention and told me to go up to my room to pack my things. In about fifteen minutes I met her in the large entryway where we used to stand to have our comb and hankie check before school. She reminded me to get my cornet out of the hall closet. In tears, she hugged me and asked me if I really wanted to leave the school. I told her I did, and that was it. We walked out toward the back entrance where the car was waiting.

While I had been packing several of the boys had meandered down to the unit to find out what was going on. When they saw that I was leaving I could tell they were sad, but actually, I found it hard to feel their pain. I slowly walked around and shook each of their hands and said my goodbyes. It was a hard thing to do. I knew that everyone of them had dreams like I did, but unfortunately, this was my day not theirs. A few minutes later as we pulled away, I felt for the first time since that fateful day in Waterville, that my life had just taken a huge turn for the better. It was a feeling I have never forgotten. For the first time in three long childhood years, it seemed like the sun was shining again.

We stayed in a local hotel that night, and made the drive back to Cleveland the next day. As we pulled up to the William's street and into their driveway, I knew that this was not going to be a typical foster home. They lived in a beautiful house in an exclusive subdivision made up of private and wealthy homeowners. The grounds were beautiful, and everything about it was really nice. My new family seemed very welcoming and interested in making me feel at home. They had two sons and two daughters. Tim, the youngest son was my age, and Jim the older son was my brother's age. Jim and Geoff were in high school together and both on the football team. Jim was the top running back in the league. Their two girls were Jill, who was about nine or ten years-old, and Jackie who was about five. In just a short time, Tim and I became immediate friends.

It was only a few weeks till Labor Day, so in just a day or so, Mrs. Williams took Tim and me out for school clothes shopping. The boy's school could only provide me with a minimal amount of clothing to take from the school since it was official school property. I didn't mind because that meant I got to buy almost a whole new wardrobe for school, and Mrs. Williams told me to pick out whatever I wanted. It was a lot different than what I had been used to. Among the best things I got were two new pairs of jeans. As soon as we got home Tim and I went to the washing machine to "bleach" them. Then we tie-dyed a couple of plain t-shirts we had just bought. It was the summer of 1969, and almost every kid on the block was doing exactly the same thing. Within a few days, I had met about four or five of Tim's school friends, and we started hanging out together. Most nights we went to the park and played football and stuff. The guys really liked me and went out of their way to show me a good time. They knew my brother, and that made it possible for me to fit in easily.

One of the best things about being out of Milton Hershey School was the fact that I was looking forward to going to a coed school in a few short weeks. It didn't take the guys long to introduce me to some of the girls in our eighth grade class. They thought it was funny that I hadn't been around girls for the last two years, so they made sure that I was involved in playing a few late summer games of spin the bottle before school started. In just a few weeks my eighth grade year began at the Chagrin Falls Middle School, and I was a wild and aggressive teenager who believed that there was nothing ahead but sunshine and hope, and I wasn't going to allow myself to be disappointed in either one.

Most of that aggressive behavior came out after school or while playing sports, but I had a definite discipline problem in certain classroom environments. For instance, my gym teacher, Mr. McGilvary, was a strict disciplinarian type of guy. He was fine as long as you followed his rules; if you broke them there was a price to pay for it. Most of the time punishment involved extra laps, push-ups, or something similar. But on several occasions I would be in his office for corporal punishment. Most of the boys feared this more than anything, but for some reason I actually got to enjoy it. You have to understand, at the boy's school corporal punishment by spanking was routine. It happened all the time.

All the professors at Catherine Hall had a big menacing paddle in their schoolroom closets. Some of them were big and broad and had holes drilled in the paddle part. Others might be a little more rounded like an oversize ping-pong paddle. There were at least two professors who chose two paddles with springs mounted between them. The idea was that when you received one good swat, you would actually get two for the price of one. In the sixties, spanking was still the norm, and most schools paddled for bad behavior. When you get spanked as much as I did, you simply got used to it. For me, I was able to tolerate quite a bit of pain. Consequently, I loved it when Mr. McGilvary called me into his office for one of his whippings. He would say, "Bend over bud and touch your toes." I would smile, quickly obey, and then take three hard ones. Then I would stand back up and give him the biggest grin you ever saw.

I think Mr. McGilvary thought I was a lunatic. I also had him for study hall every day at two-o'clock in the cafeteria. There were probably about a hundred students in there for study hall, and the rules were simple. You did your homework and whispered quietly to your neighbor if you had to speak. If you talked loud or anything else you were made to come up to his make-shift desk area and get in the push-up position in front of the class. This would last until study hall was dismissed. I spent the vast majority of every study hall my entire school year in the push-up position. For me it gave me two simple things. First, I loved the challenge of not collapsing before the bell rang, and second, I loved the attention I got from it. Attention-getting was my way of saying I needed to be noticed.

I think what I really wanted was someone to take time to talk to me, ask me about my life, my family, and my hopes. Even my new family didn't satisfy that need in me. They hardly ever talked to me about my life or took time to ask me what had happened to my family or why I had ended up orphaned. In fact, from the day I left my stepmother, sister, and brother, hardly anyone ever asked me anything about what had happened or why. Perhaps in those days, they thought it might be too traumatic to even bring it up. It was never talked about, but deep down, I desperately needed to talk about these things. More than that, I needed someone with the people skills to know how to reach my heart. Unfortunately this didn't happen, and it would be a long time before that would ever come to pass.

Before I knew it, my eighth grade year came to a close, and my first full summer as a teenager had arrived. These lazy days of summer were filled with summer jobs to provide pocket money, make-up football games, sleepovers, and the typical shenanigans of teen-age boys. Going into ninth grade meant that me and my other friends would be going to the high school the next year and this meant certain initiations into the full teenage-life. At least that's what we thought.

One night we got someone to buy us a case of beer,

and we camped in the woods, built a big fire, and got roaring drunk. We repeated this again toward the end of July when Tim's parents were vacationing in Cape Cod. That night we had lots of beer and several girls attended, but this time we had it at the house. Unfortunately, the neighbor next door was impressed with neither the noise or the beer cans in his yard the next day, and we got reported when the parents returned from Massachusetts a few days later. I don't have much of a recollection of the events that followed, but in a few days, my things were packed, and I was on my way once again to my next foster home. Saying goodbye to my brother at my uncle's house was brutal. I had no idea where I was going next, and my brother couldn't intervene. The merry-go- round was spinning again, and who knew where it would stop this time.

I found out the next day as my caseworker and I drove the two-and-a- half hour trip back over to the town where I had grown up. Bowling Green held something of a nostalgic feeling for me now. I thought at least I would be back in the town where I had some sense of security and home. It wasn't long before those thoughts vanished as we drove off Route 6 and onto Napoleon Road, a few miles from my boyhood home. We turned into an old stone farmhouse, which had become a receiving home run by the state welfare system for those kids without a permanent home. I was the next one on the list and not long after arriving, my caseworker Judy left to head back into Bowling Green to go home. Once again, I felt bewildered as I sat in the living room with about six kids I had never seen before. A few others were in their rooms, and so I didn't see them until around suppertime.

The house parents were a couple I really didn't like at all. It seemed to me that they had no genuine empathy for anyone, and that they were in the "kid" business for the money. They both smoked unfiltered cigarettes, and the man would come in every other day or so with a twelve-pack of beer. I had no emotional connection with them at all, and they didn't seem to care much about my situation either. They had a son, Jesse, who was about three years older than me. He had no other siblings so he was kind of spoiled by his hillbilly mom and dad.

One day about the middle of August he asked me if I wanted to go hunting with him. Hunting to him meant he was going over by the county railroad tracks to shoot woodchucks. His .22 caliber rifle had a scope on it, so it was pretty easy to spot and shoot them. He also had a lever-action single-shot .22 caliber gun which he let me use. We went squirrel hunting one morning with both guns, and I shot my first squirrel with that twenty-two, single shot. It was the luckiest shot I ever made. The sights on this gun were so fat they completely covered up the entire target at sixty yards, but I got lucky and hit a red squirrel in the head with the first shot. The funny thing about it was the fact that the thing was so small; we couldn't even skin it to fry it. I never hit another thing with that gun the rest of the month.

Jesse also had a little motor scooter. Several nights we would go on the back of his scooter to hunt barn pigeons. All we took was a burlap bag and a flashlight. He had previously gotten permission to go into some local farmers' barns to "hunt," so we would quietly walk into the barn in pitch dark, and shine the light up into the barn rafters along the ends of the barn. The pigeons would be sitting there roosting. That first night he shined the light directly into the eyes of one hapless bird temporarily paralyzing it, and then he asked me to hold the light while he climbed up the rafters to grab the bird. It was the craziest thing I ever saw, but we would go back to the house every night with a bag full of birds. The next day we would wring their necks, clean them, and put them in their freezer.

I had been there a few weeks when I had a surprise visit one day at about noon. Into the yard drove a little yellow Volkswagen bug. I stepped out on the back porch to see my sister Lee step out of the passenger seat. This was only the second time I had seen her since fifth grade. The welfare department allowed her to come see me at the Warner's for an hour or so, not long before I left for the boy's school. On this occasion we hugged and she asked me how I was; how long I had been there, and what had been going on. She was now married. Her husband Eric held out his hand and shook my mine asking me how I was doing. I think I had a hard time taking it all in. They seemed really glad to see me, but I knew that there were restraints on the visit because they could not stay long. Lee had just dropped out of Ohio State and come back to Bowling Green and was working in a local drug store.

Eric had just returned from Viet Nam, where he had earned two purple hearts and post-traumatic stress syndrome. I didn't realize it at the time but both Eric and Lee had become heroin addicts, and I would learn later that they had also become a sort of Bonnie and Clyde couple where thievery and deception won them their daily drug needs. Eric was also a former Golden Gloves boxer with a reputation for being a tough guy with little fear. I think my hillbilly house-parents had been told to limit the visit because before we could enter into any meaningful conversation, they had to go. My growing insecurities with life had not been helped by the visit at all; in fact, just the opposite had taken place. Now I wondered why my married sister could not have just taken me home with her. My heart went with them as they pulled away from the farmhouse on Napoleon Road. It was not until years later I would realize that going home with them would not have been a benefit to me at all.

The following week school started back. I was a ninth-grader at the Junior High School up in the middle of town. On the very first day of school, Mrs. Everton, a farm woman who lived less than quarter mile from us when we were kids, noticed me through the cafeteria kitchen window. I didn't know it, but her daughter Carol, who had been good friends with my sister as kids, was now married and lived just a few miles from my location on Napoleon Road. Just a few days later, the house parents told me that a couple who was interested in me was coming to pick me up for an evening visit. Surprisingly, just after supper Friday night, Carol and her husband Dan, pulled into the driveway, and in a few minutes I was driving with them over to their farm a few miles away. It was actually nice to get away from my bleak surroundings I was in and actually be with someone who knew me.

Carol had known our family ever since we were little kids on the farm. She rode our bus and our families were well acquainted. She had revered my father and dreamed of working for him someday in the hospital setting. She had since graduated from high school, worked jobs, dated, and finally married Dan, a schoolteacher's son from Rudolph, a nearby town. They had not yet been able to have children, so upon hearing from her mother at the Junior High that I was back in the area as a ward of the state, she and Dan thought they might offer me their home, a room and some hope.

It had been over four years since my stepmother had given up custody of us kids. A lot had changed in that time. For me, I had been in five different homes along with a school for boys. When I left my mother, brother and sister in Waterville, I was a happy, confident young boy who always had the expectation of better tomorrows. I now knew that there was no way back to those boundless, sunlit days. These last few years had been filled with loss, anger, anxiety, insecurity, and fear of what was just around the corner. My former self-assuredness had not just been shaken, it was broken. I knew what I once was and where it had all started to go down-hill, but for some reason, I couldn't reclaim it. It was like trying to put Humpty Dumpty back together again. I always thought that there would be someone — anyone — who knew who I was, where I had come from, and who I was supposed to be, and help me sort it all out.

Regrettably, it seemed like everyone who knew me had been deliberately told to never bring it up around me. I felt like I lived in some strange world where no one really knew anything about my life situation but me. I wanted to communicate my feelings, but it was too complicated for me to put into words. I was slowly being convinced that nobody could really understand my circumstances. I think I had come to the conclusion that nobody really cared. After four years, with no end in sight, I was beginning to realize the hope of getting my family back was really nothing but a fantasy. Nevertheless, I kept hoping.

I also didn't know it at the time, but the Wood County Welfare Department had another option available to them regarding my immediate future. About an hour away was a juvenile delinquent center, and evidently, I had been recommended as a good candidate as an inductee after arriving from Chagrin Falls. It seems I had become the scapegoat for having instigated the party at my former foster home. I suppose that if I had done something stupid after arriving back in Bowling Green, that juvenile detention center is where I would have ended up. I don't value dwelling on hypotheticals, but in hindsight this would have likely been the end of me. Fortunately, that never happened.

It was about a week after Dan and Carol came to take me out for their trial visit on Friday night that an invitation from them came asking if I wanted to make it permanent. I remember simply saying yes.

At fifteen years of age, I was now in my sixth foster home — and back in my place of origin.

CHAPTER SEVEN

Who Am I?

MY NEW FOSTER family had one thing different about them from the previous homes where I had been. They had some awareness of my family background that no one else had. Carol's family farm was less than a quarter mile from where I had grown up. She had been a childhood friend of my sister Lee. Her parents, like most farm families, were always ready neighbors to help when help was needed. Her dad, a WW2 vet, had known my dad, and I'm sure had offered his willing assistance when dad bought the farm in 1953. After the war, he himself had settled on his wife's family farm, raised cattle, and worked at the grain elevator in town. He would spend the next forty years working for the same company, becoming as much a part of the landscape as the dirt itself. He was one of the two farmers on hand that night who hauled my stepsister's boyfriend out of our bathroom in a drug-induced rage. I have no doubt he felt some responsibility toward me and probably had at least shared that with Carol if not Dan as well. Whatever the case, I was now living in his daughter's home where I was an orphan. At least now I was not an unknown one.

Dan and Carol had been married just over three years when I came into their lives. They had purchased an old farm about five miles southeast of her family's property. Dan was from the smaller town of Rudolph about eight miles southwest of Bowling Green. They had met shortly after high school, fallen in love, and married in 1967. By the time I arrived, they had gotten the farmhouse remodeled and ready for children. Unfortunately, they weren't immediately successful so they had to start out with a wayward fifteen year-old boy.

Since I had already started school before coming to what would be my last foster home, I decided I would do all I could to make it work. At least I was back in my hometown, and I was back among those who at least knew something of me, even if some years had passed. I thought if I pretended that nothing was really different about me now, maybe nobody would really know the difference. After all, I was still a doctor's son from a town where the local hospital still honored my last name in the pathology wing. Maybe I could just fake it, and nobody would ever be able to tell that I wasn't the same confident, self-assured kid. Time would soon tell that this was not going to work long in my favor.

That first full weekend with Dan and Carol was over before it started, and I was back at school Monday morning a somewhat bolstered young man. About the middle of that week, class elections were being announced and in the exhilaration of my new-found home-life I decided to run for president of my class. I had two opponents running for the same office, so I needed to reacquaint myself with old friends from elementary school, and make new friends as fast as I could. The following week, I got a few girls to help me with posters and we got them up around the hallways. Two weeks later the entire class met in the school auditorium for speeches before the class vote.

I knew I could make a good speech, even if I didn't believe much of what I said. I had won 2nd place in a speech contest at the boy's school in Hershey, and its memory was still fresh enough in my mind to spur me on. The speeches were made, and the vote was taken by week's end. The results would be announced on Monday morning. After the weekend passed it was back to school to learn the outcome. Election results were made over the intercom, and it was announced that I was the new president of my freshman class. I immediately began to wonder how I was going to keep all those promises I had made in the flush of my speech-making zeal. Successful bake sales, great school dances, great memories: this is what I was supposed to deliver over the course of the school year. Fortunately, we had a fairly successful class that year, but I had not been a personal success model. I happened to spend more time in the principal's office than any student in ninth grade. The school principal was constantly telling me that I needed to be an example. Fortunately, the principal was merciful most of the time. A lot of my infractions came from stupid outbursts in classes in which I had no interest. There were some kids that could get away with a lot of foolishness in school. Unluckily, I was not one of them, so I usually paid for my dumb stunts.

I had been in intramural wrestling while in eighth grade, and so I joined the freshman wrestling team early that fall. Carol worked for the athletic department at the university and would come by and pick me up after practice three days a week. The other two days I rode the bus home. I enjoyed wrestling, but I learned about the end of October, that tryouts for high school hockey were taking place out at the university ice arena. I had a few friends who I knew I had played at the boy's school and encouraged me to play, so that was the end of wrestling for me. Looking back, it was probably a timely mistake. I was not a stand-out hockey player, but I likely would have been a stand-out wrestler. Whatever the case, I would play high school hockey for the next four years. I also would have been a much better baseball player, but every spring we played in the State High School Hockey Tournaments. So I ended up playing hockey and football. Football would have to wait until my sophomore year.

I realized early on during my freshman year that my early family reputation was no longer going to be a help to me. First of all, nobody knew my family anymore. My sister had not even graduated from the local high school. The county welfare department had placed her in a foster home in southern Michigan, just over the Ohio border, where she graduated in 1968. She was accepted at Ohio State University in the summer of 1968 and began classes in the fall. Unlike Geoff, who sometimes didn't want his little brother bothering him, Lee showed me a big sister's patience. I had always had a good relationship with my sister. I could talk with her about anything, and she always helped me to think more profoundly than my little adolescent mind was capable. One of my favorite memories of growing up with her was doing dishes after dinner. We always had the local AM radio station playing, and whenever Ray Orbison's "Pretty Woman" came on, she would let me turn it up and we would sing it together, laughing when I got the words wrong.

Lee's teachers in elementary school had always commented on her grade report that she was a "gifted" student, with "brilliant" prospects, and she had an IQ of just under 150. She dropped out of Ohio State after her second year and came back to Bowling Green. While working at the pharmacy, she eventually met Eric in a bar one night after his return from Viet Nam. By all reports, they were immediately attracted to each other.

My brother Geoff finished high school in Chagrin Falls before I started my sophomore year in high school. Geoff had lived all of his high school years with our Uncle Jim and Aunt Marcia. Jim had graduated from Yale with a degree in English and taught English at the Hawken School for boys just outside Cleveland. This timely move for Geoff undoubtedly saved him from a lot of heartache during his teen years in high school. At MHS, before being taken out, he had already begun to manifest a nasty disposition toward his housefather, resulting in a fistfight. This would have only gotten worse had he been forced to stay there longer. It was undoubtedly fortunate that our Uncle Jim spared him. I always thought it odd that they didn't bring Geoff by my unit to say goodbye the day they picked him up. Maybe, in some way that was providential, too. It, no doubt, would have crushed my fragile hopes.

Geoff was able to have an almost completely normal life with our aunt and uncle. He wrestled, played football, and became interested in pottery on the side. His pottery instructor believed Geoff to have had tremendous potential as a potter. Despite his hopeful situation, in his final year of high school, he began to manifest a rebellious attitude toward Aunt Marcia almost resulting in being asked to leave their house. Fortunately, he was able to make things work until graduation, and then he was gone. Where? Few people knew or could keep track. It was the summer before my sophomore year in high school, and I never heard from him or anything about him that entire summer or fall. I later found out he had gone out to California, got into the drug scene, and completely dropped out of sight. He never told me much about that period of his life in later years. Later that semester, just after Christmas, he showed up at Lee and Eric's house. We all went skating one night down on the river at our old farm property. I didn't see him again until late that following summer.

Geoff could be unpredictable. He had my Dad's brains but was extremely temperamental. I didn't understand it at the time, but he, too, was unable to process what our stepmother had done to us. His bitterness wasn't on the surface like mine. He wore it differently. Because of it, he was unable to make long-term commitments in virtually any area of life. He was the kind of guy that could be there one day and then gone the next. His level of non-conformity was also astounding to most people. During my last few years of high school he lived in a barn in which he constructed a living space for himself. All of this strange behavior would moderate in later years, but the commitment to reach his potential never materialized. I never saw this completely until years later.

Our family's lack of continuity, along with my "orphan" status kept me in a cloud of uncertainty with most town folks. It was always better for them not to ask questions about me than to be made uncomfortable by the answers. Consequently, I usually had two strikes against me before I ever got to the plate with those considered respectable. It always seemed that every new situation I encountered was just another proving ground for me. I think I decided somewhere during my sophomore year that I was not very good at playing that game anymore. At another time in my life, at a better time, I would have relished such opportunities, but now it seemed more like mockery to me.

This would be a major turning point in my attitude that would affect me throughout the rest of high school. I simply decided that if people didn't care about me, I would just up the ante and be angry toward them for no reason. By the end of my freshmen year, along with my class presidency, I was now getting ready for a troubled sophomore experience at the high school. But with my first year behind me, the summer of 1971 had now arrived.

Dan and Carol's home was out east of town on the very edge of the school district. Without a car, I spent most of the summer in the country. That summer before starting high school, I baled hay for pocket cash. It was really the easiest way to make extra money, especially without personal transportation. Usually some of my friends who lived in town would do it, too. One day a farmer called our house looking for some help baling his hay fields. I called a few friends, and, in an hour or so, I met them at a house a few miles from our farm. This particular farmer had a hired hand named Lundy that had worked for him for years. I don't know where Lundy came from, but he was a huge individual with massive arms and chest. He was getting old, but you could tell he was still able to work. He unloaded the wagons on to the elevator, which fed the hay bales up to the upper loft in the barn. He hardly ever spoke, and at the beginning of every new wagonload he just looked up at you and started pitching bales. He would seldom stop for any reason, including our exhaustion.

Lundy had an interesting past. The story about him was as strange as he seemed to be. It was said that as a much younger man he had killed his wife in a fit of jealous rage. He had evidently done his time in prison and now spent his lonely days as a farm hand. He had also trained horses in his younger life. The farmer told us he was the only man he'd ever seen who could jerk a horse down to its knees. We never knew if the story about Lundy was true, but he could outwork every one of us boys. He never stopped the elevator until the wagon was empty. It didn't matter to him if we were buried up in the mound; he just kept them coming all day long and nobody dared say a word.

On our second job that summer, we were baling hay

for a farmer closer to town, and a couple of my hockey buddies came out to make some extra cash. The arrangement was for the most inexperienced guys to work on the lower loft. I was in the upper level, which required me to have a baling hook to hook and grab the bail as the middle guy lifted it up. We were about halfway through the load in a good rhythm when the middle guy threw the bale up and lost control of it just as I was reaching down to hook the bail that wasn't quite there. Unfortunately his arm was, and I hooked him right in his left forearm. He screamed bloody murder and in a few minutes the farmer was on the way to the hospital with him. Fortunately they returned about an hour later with the good news that the hook had only penetrated the top fatty layer of flesh on top of the muscle requiring only a few stitches. He was lucky, and I was relieved. We all thought it was pretty funny, and so after a few good laughs we finished the day's work. My city slicker friend now had a great farm story with wounds and all to tell our mutual friends.

Just after the fourth of July, high school football tryouts started. Most of us sophomores knew we had an uphill battle trying to get any kind of a starting position. In our case, there was at least one upperclassman who would go on to play for the university. There were some big, fast, and pretty tough players. I was about five foot seven and weighed in at a massive 145 lbs, but I had two things going for me. I was fast, and I loved collisions. So my coaches ended up starting me on the kick-off team. For the duration of July we had two practices a day, then in August three-a- day practices started. Being in football country, it was all pretty serious business at our high school.

About the third week in August we were getting ready for a scrimmage game with another school before Labor Day weekend. About the middle of that week, Carol called me to the phone. It was my stepmother on the other line. I was a little surprised to hear from her and wondered why she had called. I hadn't seen or talked to her in over five years. She had never bothered to come see me at the boys' school, and as far as I knew, she couldn't have cared less about me anymore. All of sudden she's on the phone asking me if I would like to come visit her on the weekend. It was kind of strange looking back on it, but I think in my juvenile mind, I hoped that she really loved me after all. Maybe the last five years were just a bad blip on the radar screen of life or something. Who could know? Anyway, I told her I would come, and so Friday night after school, she and her new husband Harold picked me up at the farm.

They lived in Waterville—the same town we lived in after moving from the farm—and so the drive through town and then on to Waterville brought back some poignant memories with my siblings from years back. They lived in a nice upper-middle class neighborhood, and their house indicated that they lived on a different level than the one in which I was presently living. There were no barns, pigs, or horses. Their back-yard was fenced with a beautiful swimming pool just off the patio. Her husband Harold was a bank builder, and he evidently was pretty successful. That Friday night as I slept in the guest room, I wondered how different things might have been if that morning in Waterville had never happened the way it did. What if I had just come down those stairs that morning in early August to breakfast like normal? What if my stepmom had told me she loved me that morning and given me a warm hug instead of a cold good-bye? What if I had started back to school that fifth grade year, gone trick or treating that Halloween, had Christmas alongside my brother and sister, and played baseball again that spring? Would I be a different person now? I thought I knew the answer to those questions, but I didn't like the answers I heard in my head, because it didn't matter now.

I woke the next morning to the unfamiliar sounds of a strange household. My stepmother was in her kitchen making breakfast for Harold and me. I got up and dressed to go out to the kitchen. My stepmother greeted me with a good morning that made me realize that this was really only going to be a visit. She was trying too hard to be nice, but being a mother doesn't require that kind of effort, and I instinctively knew it. She had made eggs and toast. In a few minutes Harold appeared, and we all sat down to eat breakfast. Now that I realized that this was not going to be the first step in my return to the family home, breakfast took on a somewhat different feel. It's strange when you know where home is, and it isn't where your "mother" lives.

After breakfast, I went out into the back yard to play with the dog and look around. Both Harold and my stepmom came out and we ended up sitting by the pool for a while and talking. I don't remember now what we talked about, but I'm sure I would have had it been memorable. I do remember telling mom that I would need to be taken into town later that afternoon to get ready for the high school scrimmage. It was a big night for me because I would be starting on the kick-off team as a sophomore. To me and my friends, that was big stuff, and I wasn't about to be late. The game was at seven o'clock and I asked mom to take me in to the park to meet my friends at around four-thirty. We would take our time and then head over to the locker room around five-thirty or so. Either way, mom and Harold would have to make the twenty-five minute drive twice. They would return home and then come back for the game at seven. I was excited that I had real family coming that night to see me play.

Harold may have achieved success as a bank builder, but any professional successes were dampened by his alcoholism. It was shortly before noon when he mixed drinks for both my stepmother and himself. By the time we left to drive into town later that afternoon, Harold had been in the sauce fairly steadily. My stepmother wasn't far behind. I could tell when we got in the car to leave for the park that their personal routine was being interrupted. They didn't say anything, but they didn't have to, I knew that I was becoming an imposition by having to go earlier to the game than they did. Any parent with kids would know that when kids play sports, it requires playing taxi. Unfortunately, neither one of them understood that sort of commitment. After dropping me off at the park, I was now hoping, not really assured, that they would come back to see me play at game time.

We kicked off that night, and I started on the right side of the kick-off team. I was one of four sophomore players who would letter that year. It was a proud moment for me and those other lucky teammates of mine who shared the honors. At half time we crowded into the locker room to hear from our coaches and make mid-game adjustments when another player told me someone was outside asking for me. I went out to see that my stepmother and Harold were standing there. Speaking for both of them, my stepmother told me that they didn't know that my staying with them would require them driving into town twice in one day, and being tired, that they would have to go home now. By this time, I could smell that they reeked of booze, and I now knew what I had suspected for five years. My stepmother couldn't be bothered with me, and definitely did not want to be involved in my life, and over the course of that August weekend, she had made it abundantly clear. That door to the past, which I had left cracked open just in case, was now shut and locked for good. When I went back into the locker room a moment later, I was just a little harder than before, with less light in my soul. Something else would happen later that year, which would confirm that decision, but that will have to wait.

Just a few weeks later school started back. Being in the high school was definitely a step up. I enjoyed being in a larger pool of kids and losing some of the narrowed focus of junior high. Having made the football team, there was a small bit of earned respect among my peers. I wasn't class president that year, but I wasn't really interested in being a leader anymore. For one thing, since the stepmother incident, I was no longer able to conceal my disposition like before. My last vestige of hope in getting my family back was no longer there. In its place I felt more vulnerable and insecure than ever, and it was difficult to mask. I now felt I had to protect myself from further hurt, and that allowed me to justify anger and occasional rage. Consequently, I built a wall between myself and my world and just went through the motions. I watched my friends and schoolmates growing up in high school, but I felt like I was somewhere else. I saw their moms and dads involved in their lives. I saw them grounded in family life with parents, siblings — with predictable outcomes. I felt like a forty year-old man in a fifteen year-old boy's body. I had seen more life come and go than most of those at school could even imagine. As a result, I lost my ability to identify with them, and so that school year I chose older friends, and consequently more risky behavior. We all played football, but when we weren't practicing or playing on Friday nights, we spent our leisure time looking for trouble, and we usually found it.

As football season ended, hockey followed right on its heels. We practiced at five-thirty in the morning three mornings a week up at the university arena. For me, it was tough. It was my job to feed and water the horse every day before school. When the pigs were being born in the middle of winter, I had to make sure they were fed and the heat lamps were working before leaving for practice. Because I lived way out of town, I had to depend on my foster parents to take me to practice or rely on a few teammates' willingness to come out and pick me up. I absolutely hated depending on other people. It only served to reinforce the vulnerability and weakness I already felt inside and, subsequently, the anger at my circumstances. There were few places I could express my feelings and far fewer people who even knew what was going on inside me. One day at school, an upperclassman stuck his leg out to trip me during a study hall in the cafeteria. Instead of ignoring his immature gesture and moving on, I reacted by hitting him with a chair. I was suspended for three days from school. Several weeks later, when I was at my locker one afternoon, I took offense at an innocent statement a student made to me, and I punched him until he fell down in the stairwell. I was again suspended.

All the while my sister and her husband Eric were living with his parents in town and were hopelessly addicted to heroin. They would do most anything to maintain their expensive habits of up to two hundred dollars day. There were a few times they involved me by asking me to return stolen merchandise to stores they had visited. In December, 1971, right around Christmas, their supply of heroin had evidently dried up. Eric drove their yellow VW to Toledo to rob a pharmacy of their supply of Dilaudid, a morphine-based derivative drug.

When entering a store he would usually loiter around the toiletries section for a while waiting for the pharmacy counter to empty of customers. With a tire iron inserted in his jacket sleeve, he would then walk to the counter and tell the pharmacist why he was there, and that if he wanted to go home to his wife after work, he should do exactly what he told him to do. Usually, Lee would drive getaway, but on this occasion Eric was working by himself. The pharmacist easily complied that night and Eric left the store, ran around the corner, got in his car, made it to the freeway and was heading for home when he saw flashing lights behind him. Just before leaving the city limits on Route 75, a cruiser had approached him from the rear and pulled him over for a simple taillight violation. Thinking that he was being pulled over for the robbery, Eric turned the car to the shoulder and reached in the back seat for his rifle. He hadn't intended to be caught. Fortunately, while the officer approached the car, Eric got the gun jammed between the door and the back seat. He told me later that before he had scuffled with the policeman, he had planned on killing him with the gun, but with it jammed between the seats, he chose to just shove as many of the stolen pills in his mouth as he could swallow. A cheap high was as good as it was going to get. He wound up spending the holidays in jail, and was finally sentenced in early spring to ten to twenty-five years in the Ohio State Penitentiary in Mansfield, Ohio. He would have to do at least three years before he would be eligible for parole consideration. Obviously, our small-town newspaper highlighted Eric's unfortunate story. His was a life of promise gone horribly wrong.

Unfortunately, these family connections at this point in my life only served to further alienate me from the people whose respect I thought I needed. I had now completely crossed the bridge from the respectable position of a local doctor's son, to being a brother-in-law to a local drug addict turned criminal and brother to his drug-addicted wife and accomplice. It's one thing for people to have unspoken doubt about you. It's another thing all together when you give up inside and accept their verdict. As the school year dragged into the spring of '72, I found myself slowly beginning to unravel inside. I accepted the fact that things would likely never get much better, that my family was fractured beyond my ability to do anything about it, and the constant exertion attempting to change it was not worth the effort.

My realization the previous summer that my stepmother had completely rejected me was the push that had begun my downhill trajectory. But something else cemented this about Easter of that spring. We were gathered at Carol's parents for Easter dinner. They lived less than half a mile from my family home where I had lived with my dad. Just after we had finished dinner that afternoon, I was looking at some things in an old hutch drawer in their kitchen when I came across a current copy of the Wood County plot book. A plot book lists the location and owner of all the privately owned properties in a county. In farm country that you've grown up in, it's a pretty easy thing to follow. My dad owned two hundred fifty acres of some of the best river-bottom land in the county, two complete farms on opposite corners of the acreage, and one smaller home at the farthest end of the triangular shaped plot. As a boy I had played all over this pastureland. My brother and I had rope swings down next to the sheep shelter over the river. We had rafted on it with the hired hand in the summer days as kids. We had ridden shotgun on the green Oliver tractor hauling manure from the horse stables all over those corn, oat, and wheat fields. We knew every mulberry tree, every walnut tree, and every rock and gopher hole. My dad had left all of this real estate, the houses, outbuildings, and any other private holdings he was in possession of at the time of his death to his three children, Lee Snavely, Geoffrey Snavely, and Bruce Snavely to be held in a life estate by our stepmother until her natural death. A local attorney in town was the executor of the probated will which was signed and filed in the county court September 20, 1962. How the local attorney and my stepmother accomplished circumventing a probated will was their secret, but however they did it, it was "legal." My stepmother had actually been the one who bought the farm the year we moved to Waterville.

I had already heard from my brother and sister that our stepmother had somehow gotten our father's inheritance for herself, but the implications of it hadn't yet dawned on me entirely. As I looked at large sections of the property, which I had walked as a boy listed in the plot book that Easter Sunday, I also noticed that several of them were no longer owned by my stepmother. In fact, the attorney who was the executor of dad's will was now listed as the owner of one of the tracts of land belonging to my dad.

As I stood there in my old neighbor's kitchen, I felt like someone had stuck a knife in my gut. My sixteen year-old naiveté was being replaced with a sobering grown-up reality, one I didn't quite know how to handle emotionally. The only thing I knew to do was to be angry. The problem was that there was no way to relieve it. I couldn't go talk to anybody about it. I couldn't just take it back. There was no one who even appeared to know or care. There was simply nothing that I could do about it. There seemed to be no one who knew what had happened anyway and if they did, they didn't care enough to get involved. Hostility toward those who had wronged me had now become my new motivation for getting out of bed in the morning. I was now forced to find a new life purpose beyond getting my family and inheritance back, and being angry at the world was about the best I could do.

CHAPTER EIGHT

Sowing to the Wind

I DON'T KNOW if anyone noticed a change in me that Easter Sunday, but something had definitely changed. It was no longer just my stepmother that was the object of my seething, but the lawyer too had now become someone else to loathe. It appeared that what had happened to me and my siblings now had some context. It had all the appearances of pre-meditation and planning. I was beginning to understand that we had not been the victims of mere circumstances and unfortunate events. The very people who my father had intended to protect us from such horrors had victimized us.

The realization of this kind of thing is overwhelming for any sixteen year-old. You can take it all in mentally, but it's impossible to handle emotionally, and I was no exception. For me it would soon involve destructive behavior that endangered everything in my life, including life itself. Somehow, I had crossed an invisible line, which I had no idea was even there. As that spring turned to the summer before my junior year in high school, I deliberately began to purposefully live life on the dangerous edges. I felt that I had less to lose than ever before.

June had hardly gotten in gear when I had one of my football friends from town sleep over at the farm. Jack and I decided to "camp out" in the barn and about midnight we took off and headed toward town. To shorten our trek we took a direct route through farmer's fields to stay off the main roads. My friend's dad was a member of the local country club, so we decided we would break into the golf clubhouse and steal some really good golf clubs and then try to sell them later somewhere else to avoid being tied to the robbery. Everything went off without a hitch. The clubs and expensive bag were stashed in the club's wooded area to be picked up just after the weekend. We traveled the fields most of the way back until we finally hitched a ride with some older teens out smoking weed on the country roads. They offered us some and by the time they dropped us off near the house, we were lucky to find our way back to the barn. By the time we got up the next morning, we had almost forgotten the previous night's escapades, but unfortunately that wouldn't last for very long.

The summer days were pretty boring for a rebellious teenager. I always had chores to do, but I didn't know what to do with myself most of the time. An old acquaintance of my foster family had sold me his old Cushman motor scooter for fifty dollars, so for couple of weeks I worked on it and got it going. Other than that, Dan would often give me jobs to do around the farm to keep me busy, like cleaning the horse stalls or the pig shed. I resented having to be by myself stuck out in the country while all my city friends were free to do what they wanted. I took as many hay baling jobs as I could, but that always depended on the weather being dry enough to bale. Nobody would put damp bales in the barn because of the fear of fire. The molding of damp hay could raise the temperature of a hay bale enough to create spontaneous combustion, so unless it was an extremely dry summer, it just wasn't a steady summer job.

Consequently, I couldn't buy a car to go anywhere without my friends picking me up or asking my foster parents for a ride, and I just hated to ask. They both worked and I knew when they pulled in the driveway after work, they didn't look forward to leaving again until the next day. I always thought they assumed it normal for a farm kid to be happy on the farm. That was the way they grew up. I just wasn't one of those kids anymore. I was really looking forward to late July when football practice would start again. It wasn't long after practices had started that I got some bad news that one of our own high school girls had been killed in a car accident a few days earlier. It just so happened that I had gotten interested in her before school had gotten out in June, and now suddenly she was gone. It took me by complete surprise. After all, when you are a teenager, you think you and all your young friends are next to invincible. That illusion made it difficult for me to accept her sudden death.

Three-a-day practices had just started in August, and I decided I would go by the funeral home after the morning practice was over to see her before the scheduled afternoon viewing when I would be at practice. Everybody at the funeral home knew our family, and I went to school with one of the owner's kids, so I was sure Mrs. Hanneford would allow me in to pay my respects during off hours. I knocked on the back door of the funeral home, and Mrs. Hanneford herself came to the door. She gladly let me in after I reminded her who I was and why I had come. I thought she might not be prepared for what I was asking but she showed me the parlor where Kelly's body was located and told me I could stay as long as I wanted. She pointed the way out, and then headed off to another area of the funeral home. There was one single light left on in the room over Kelly's body and as I approached the casket I couldn't get out my mind that it was just weeks earlier we were standing at the entrance to the high school talking. Now there she was with one single daisy in her clasped, lifeless hands. I walked up to the casket and looked at her face and began to talk. I don't remember what I said to her, but I'll never forget the utter emptiness in that room. I was not prepared to face death that morning. I didn't know why she was gone, where she was, or any other answers to my questions. In a moment, I turned around and walked away—finding the back door, I quickly let myself out. I realized that although I had faced death with my own father, I still hadn't seriously considered life after death, and that made looking into that girl's face that morning pretty eerie.

I hadn't seriously considered death before then. I was too young when my father had died. As far as religion went, it seemed to me to be no more than a formal human response to the unknown, done in the confines of a church or funeral home. If there was some truth I was missing and needed to know, I wasn't interested or ready to find it out. At home, I was forced to go to church on Sunday morning down the road at the country Methodist church, but I was only interested in a few of the girls who also came out of obligation. I thought the church stuff was for old ladies and farmers who traded in their overalls for a suit every Sunday. In hindsight, I guess I thought I was invincible too, but the school year would begin shortly and I would soon find out I wasn't.

The beginning to the fall semester in high school was the "Big Burn" on Friday following Labor Day. It was the school pep rally commencing the new school year and the football season. There were high hopes that year for the football team. We had a tough league roster, but we had some good players who had big expectations. Unfortunately, we would go on to play the worst season the school had for some time. We actually earned the right to play in what was infamously called "The Toilet Bowl" at the end of the season to determine who took last place honors in the league. The high hopes for a good season hadn't panned out.

To make matters worse, about midway through the season, I was called in for an appointment at the welfare department after school. I was informed by one of the directors that the previous summer's break-in at the Country Club had been reported, and that I had been indicated by my accomplice who had been discovered with the stolen merchandise. I was placed on probation for breaking and entering and told not to have any further contact with my accomplice friend. Jack told me himself at school the next week that his parents absolutely insisted that he have absolutely nothing to do with me, and that's the way it was for the rest of the year, in fact for the next two years of high school. I didn't know it at the time, but our friendship might have been the only thing that saved me from being sent to the juvenile detention center in Van Wert, Ohio. Had I acted alone, I likely would have been sent up by the Juvenile Court, but because my accomplice's father was an upstanding local citizen and member of the Country Club, I was spared the worst. They didn't press charges, and I received probation at the hands of the welfare department. My only punishment was that I had to report to my caseworker once a month that entire school year. Considering who I was, and what I had done, it was once again fortunate that I had gotten off so lucky.

Just a week or so after football was over, hockey practices began. We played several games prior to Christmas break and then it was time for a two-week vacation. I was spending a lot more of my down time with city friends those days, so the break wasn't as boring as the previous two years on the farm. A few of my friends had cars, and we would go into town and play pool at the local pool hall. By the time Christmas day had come and gone, we were looking forward to celebrating New Year's Eve by crashing some college parties and such around town. My foster parents were scheduled to be gone themselves until the wee hours of the morning, so I basically didn't have to worry about what time I had to be home. My friends picked me up about seven-thirty and we drove around and drank wine in the car for a couple hours before we decided that we would visit a few parties around town. Some of them were going ok but weren't really that exciting, so we left to go see a few girl friends. I wanted to see a girl who I had been seeing during the first term before Christmas. I wasn't sure of where we stood because we hadn't been talking for a couple of weeks. I didn't know it but she had moved on without telling me what was happening.

When we drove by her house that night in a semi-drunken condition, I saw that there was an unfamiliar car in the driveway. I knocked on the door anyway, and after a few minutes Carrie came to door and told me to come back some other time because she had company. I could see that she was in the living room with a really big guy who I found out later was a star basketball player from out of town. I lost my temper upon seeing him and ripped down all of the Christmas lights around her door in an attempt to get him to come outside. It didn't work, so I just left and got back in the car with my buddies. They drove around the block for a few minutes and when we got back to her house, I saw him just getting into his car in the driveway, so I thought I would scare him before I got a chance to talk to Carrie. I didn't realize it, but this girl wanted nothing to do with me. I quickly got out and ran to his car and tried to open his car door and drag him out. The doors were locked, so I began beating on the car window attempting to break it when the neighbor man next door, hearing the commotion, came out and met me in the yard. This distraction enabled my basketball friend to pull out and speed off, but now I was in a heated argument with another total stranger. I didn't know the man himself, but I went to school with his son. He yelled, "You need to get out of here right now!" I told him I wanted to talk with Carrie. He repeated what he said before. Then I told him if he didn't get out my way, I'd kill him. Then I heard a few more doors open and more yard lights appearing, and I thought the next phase would be the police, so I turned and walked away.

Down the street a few blocks away my friends found me, and we left the neighborhood for another party. I never gave it another thought until the next morning. The rest of the night consisted of more drinking, some sexual escapades with female strangers, and a late night trip home with a college girl in a snowstorm. It was after three in the morning when I got home, and my foster parents were still not home yet. So I climbed the stairs up to my room and knew nothing until I heard the phone ring about eight o'clock in the morning. It was Carol telling me that they stayed the night at their friends because of the storm. Almost as soon as I hung up the phone, it rang again. This time it was the son of Mr. Roone, the neighbor I had threatened the night before. He told me that his dad said that if I didn't come to his house and give him a full explanation for my behavior last night with an apology included, the incident would likely become a police record. I didn't want this on my juvenile record, so I told him I'd come in a few days. Of course, I didn't have a choice. For all I knew that could be the proverbial straw that broke the camel's back for me getting sent to the detention center.

On Tuesday, after practice, I went to see Mr. Roone.

We sat in his family room, and I told him I was sorry for making the threat on his life. He seemed totally incredulous that a young seventeen year-old could utter such things and really mean them. I thought of his son, the one I saw in the halls between classes. I could see what he meant. His son was perfectly normal, from a good home with two loving natural parents, a good student, with a fairly predictable life ahead of him. As his father, to even think of this son uttering such threats seemed totally bizarre, but for me, it seemed entirely justified. Maybe I thought he was just another hindrance to my quest for love, even if only seventeen year-old love. I couldn't tell Mr. Roone of my jaundiced perceptions there, but I was thinking them the whole time. Despite the situation, I told him I regretted what I said, and that I said it in the height of passion with no regard for reality. I never really got the impression that he understood my explanation. He just sort of went through the motions of accepting it. After several minutes, he gradually led me to the door and told me he hoped that nothing like this would ever happen again. I of course told him it wouldn't and quietly left through the front door. Somehow once again, I had dodged another bad behavior bullet that could have changed my life for the worst. Looking back, it was truly another blessing I didn't recognize then, but regrettably, it wouldn't be the last.

From the beginning of my freshman year until then, things had devolved in a number of ways. Whereas I had attempted to hide my unsavory side by running for class president and basically pretending I was still the doctor's son, I was no longer able to play that game on any level. The personal confidence I once possessed was no longer there, and I was running on an empty reputation. All anybody knew about me now I had either manufactured myself or on the reputation of being a welfare kid. Another thing, which set me apart from the jock crowd, was the fact that being an athlete meant living by sort of an acceptable moral code, and I absolutely detested the idea of trying to please somebody, even if it was within reason. I was reminded of this when I lettered in football as a sophomore. This automatically gave you membership in the Key Club at our high school, but I was never asked to come to meetings or reminded of my status. Because of my reputation, the message that I wasn't wanted in the club was loud and clear, so I never even bothered. I figured that if that's what people thought of me, I would go ahead and prove they were right about their assessment. Looking back now, I was taking the easy way out. Instead of bucking the tide of bad breaks and lowered expectations with uncharacteristic moral fiber, I gave in to the worst.

I remember wanting nothing but my family back, and the feeling of my brother and sister sitting beside me at the dinner table. But every day that went by was a reminder that I was living somewhere in a past that would never happen again.

Just a few months after Christmas that year in 1973, it was all even further away than ever. One of my hockey buddies at the ice arena handed me a copy of the local newspaper after practice one night, and I saw my sister's picture alongside a headline on the front page for being involved in an attempted murder. For a moment I stood there stunned, and then it dawned on me how disjointed this whole thing really was. Normally, I would have known of this tragedy before anyone else. Every family knows that. Families support each other and act as buffers between their loved ones and the cruelties of a cold, indifferent world—but not in my family's world. Nobody ever called me, or even stopped to think that this girl accused of murder was my big sister. She too, was a doctor's daughter, a brilliant girl, and a young woman with three times as much future ahead of her than life lived. Now a debased shell of wasted potential, embittered by a broken home, her face in the paper revealed the anger and resentment of having been exploited by a greedy lawyer and a truly wicked stepmother. She obviously had never gotten over it or found anything in life more important than an earthly inheritance. She had allowed herself to be crushed by the loss of her loving father and the subsequent abandonment of a once-trusted stepmother as well as an unconcerned birth mother. This coupled with the forced separation from her two brothers was more than she was ever willing to accept or put behind her.

She was tried later in March and incarcerated for a full year at the Marysville Woman's prison downstate for the lesser charge of aiding and abetting a shooting. Lee and her two accomplices had staged the sexual blackmail of a businessman in her own apartment. Her male accomplice shot the man during the staged debacle and nearly killed him. Fortunately, he lived, and long prison sentences were averted. Lee would get paroled the following Christmas if she established good prison behavior for the duration. I could only hope for that, and I did. I wanted the chance for her to see me play hockey the next year, and watch me graduate in 1974. Then we could rent a house somewhere together with Geoff and begin the process of catching up. Even Geoff had talked to Lee about doing something similar in Cleveland. That hope to recapture family was still burning in all our hearts.

Small town life can be very unforgiving. There is simply no way to hide from the fact that half your family is in the penitentiary. Everybody at school knew it, at least I thought so. Despite that fact, I visited Lee at the county jail right up to her final send-off to Marysville. On the last visit before her sentencing date, I brought her in some dope to have a final high in jail, forgetting of course, that this risk was unnecessarily stupid on both my part and hers.

She also told me where she had stashed her bag of heroin paraphernalia out on the front porch of her old apartment after the failed blackmail. She didn't want it to be found, and asked me to get rid of it for her before any investigators discovered it. Sure enough, I went over there the next afternoon after school and found it. Later that night a girlfriend and I went out in the country and threw it in a ditch. A few weeks after, Lee was finally sentenced to a year behind bars, but with good behavior, she would be out by the next Christmas.

For me, life went on in Bowling Green. I continued to pull dumb stunts, which could have either gotten me killed or thrown into a detention center for underage criminals. One night a buddy of mine and I went out into the country with his dad's loaded, automatic pistol. We decided that we would rob this liquor store since it was out of town, and we were convinced that the gun would help get us some easy money. About eight o'clock one night in early February, we walked into the empty store. The owner was the only one there, and I pushed the front door open and stepped up to the counter. I handed him a bag and told him to open the register, put the money in the bag, and he wouldn't get shot. While I was doing that my buddy silently pointed the gun at his head to emphasize my words. It seemed like a good start to a successful robbery to me. But then, the proprietor looked at me and said very slowly, "You know boys, I can shoot, too." We never did wait to find out if he was bluffing or not. We ran out the door, made our escape, and were able to laugh about it all the way back to town. Like before, it appeared that someone was looking out for me.

As spring began to appear, I was busy faking my way through school, playing hockey for the high school team, and narrowly evading trouble most days. Every year, the state high school hockey championship was held in town at the university ice arena, and just like the two previous years, we lost in double overtime to Shaker Heights. I was happy when school let out for the summer of 1973. For me, it had been a miserable year. Fortunately, I had passing grades, but I expended only enough effort to make sure I didn't fail. I couldn't imagine not at least doing that much. But something happened at the close of the school year, which caused me to think. One of my football coaches impressed upon me the need of having a good year my senior year. I don't know what it was, but I wanted to prove him right, not because he challenged me to something he wasn't sure I could do. He basically told me that he expected me to be a leader on the team next fall because he thought we might go places. Well, considering we had just won the Toilet Bowl earlier in the school year, anything would have been an improvement, but I took that remark very seriously. Over the summer, I decided to make a real effort. I started running in July and by the time two-a-day practices started, I was ahead of the getting in shape regimen. We were lifting weights twice a day and running like crazy in practice drills. The coaches seemed to have an air of expectation, and there was an intensity about practice that I hadn't seen before. By August when three-a-days began, we were beginning to see a vast improvement in the spirit of the team. The skill level was solid, but it was the teamwork, which set us apart. Everyone played unselfishly, and I think we knew then that better things lay ahead.

Because of what the coach had said to me before summer break, I was no longer acting like the same guy. I had gotten my hair cut, gotten into good shape and had established a reputation as a defensive leader. I loved hitting, and because of my speed, I could be in the opposition's backfield before a runner hit the line of scrimmage. My defensive coach made me a middle guard as a stand-up lineman. The funny thing about that was I weighed less than 150 pounds. Most players at my size and weight were playing in the defensive secondary or playing offense. I was playing across from the biggest players on every team, and I loved it. By the end of August when scrimmages were played, we began to realize how the hard work over the summer had paid off. After the first four games or so, we were considered the perennial favorites to win the league and possibly the regional crown. And as expected, we did just that. The team was rated highly in the AP state football poll, and we won a berth in the state championship. Our first game in the semi-finals was a highly rated team near Akron. They had been there many times before and had a huge size and experience advantage over the "farm" team from northwest Ohio. We ended up losing to them, but it was an experience I have never forgotten.

My grades had even improved that first term during football season. However, by the time Christmas break had arrived, I was focused on only one thing. My sister was due to be released on the 18th of December from Marysville. I had skipped school to drive down to see her in the fall before she had been released. We had looked forward to getting together for Christmas and now our chance had finally come. A few days after her release, I picked her up, and we leisurely drove out to Dan's parent's house in Rudolph for Christmas lunch. She felt a little weird because she didn't know anybody but Carol, and the circumstances didn't allow much for intimate conversation. We finally excused ourselves after a few hours, and I drove Lee back into town to her husband's parent's house. She was staying there because of the restrictions established by her parole officer. I had to go out of town the next day for a hockey tournament in Cleveland, so she asked me if she could borrow my car while I was gone. I told her that was no problem, and I kissed her goodbye telling her I would park the car at the ice arena in the morning and put the keys under the front driver's mat.

The next morning I was headed in to the ice arena about six forty-five when I hit a patch of ice and flew off the road into a barren cornfield right across the road from Carol's dad's house. I was forced to leave the car and get a ride to the arena with Bob, her dad. He was just getting ready to go to work up at the grain elevator when it happened, so it was almost like he was expecting me. Unfortunately, I couldn't keep my promise to Lee, and when I got back from Cleveland I discovered that while I was gone she had skipped parole and moved out of town.

Looking back, I'm not sure she wouldn't have taken my car with her. She had evidently gotten stir crazy at her in-law's house and decided that she needed to get her own place. However, this meant breaking parole, and this made her a fugitive. She never did call me, and by March neither Geoff nor I had heard anything from her or about her. In early April, Geoff came down from Chagrin Falls and picked me up to go on a search. We drove to an address she had sent Geoff on Broadway Street in a seedy side of Toledo. She had been staying there since the first of the year. The landlord came down when he heard us knocking and told us that Lee had left sometime around March 20th or so, and he hadn't seen her since. With nothing to go on, we had no choice but to go home wondering. The only assurance I had regarding her possible safety was a letter with no return address Lee had sent me in January indicating that she intended to disappear. It was somewhat cryptic but I think her message was intended to inform me but not alarm me about her not being available.

Geoff too, had gotten a similar letter around the first of the year, but his included her Toledo address. Lee likely assumed I would be under more demand to give up her address if pressured by a questioning parole officer in our hometown. Geoff didn't have as much potential scrutiny. Well, now I knew that Lee's legal troubles were not over, and her "free and clear" status was not here yet, if it ever would be. In fact, the cloud of uncertainty it created in my mind was unsettling. As my senior year turned towards spring in 1974, the lack of closure once again reminded me that my post-graduation reverie of sharing a house with Lee and Geoff was still only a pipe dream. The state hockey tournament came and went with somewhat predictable results. We lost in double-overtime to Shaker Heights for the fourth year in a row. A few days later, a bunch of us went to Daytona Beach for spring break. I contemplated not ever going back to finish school, but I knew with just over a month left, that would have been stupid. We did all the crazy stuff spring break stories are made of. We skipped several bills in local restaurants. On one particular evening we got chased down the beach by two waiters and a manager. Yet again we were lucky, the police didn't quite get there in time.

By the time we got back to school, we were tanned and ready to finish high school. Everybody I knew seemed to be looking past graduation and beyond. A few friends were heading down to Ohio State, but most of us were intending to scatter around and get jobs. I decided to buy a motorcycle and go to Cleveland to work with my brother in construction. I had an old Jewish friend from eighth grade who wanted me to spend the summer with him at his mother's house so the prospects for the immediate future seemed about settled. A few weeks before school got out, my brother got permission to come down and pick me up for the weekend. He was staying at a rented house in Chagrin Falls. That Friday night he invited some of his friends and a few of mine from my eighth grade year to a party there at the house. I don't have much of a memory of that night except for the fact that I started drinking a fifth of 100 proof whiskey that was in his cupboard about ten o'clock. In less than two hours I had consumed the entire bottle by drinking double shots. Between shots we were smoking weed between hot knives heated on the stove. Just after midnight, I could no longer stand up or talk coherently, so my brother left to take a few people home while I passed out in the living room. When he got back a little after one, he said I was passed out on the floor. He didn't know how much alcohol I had drunk, so he playfully rolled me over with his foot. When he did, I vomited profusely. Fortunately, for me that was a good thing. I had consumed enough alcohol to kill myself twice. Looking back, I had been spared from meeting the grim reaper. Just a few weeks later, I would undoubtedly be the most fortunate graduate of Bowling Green High School, and I wouldn't even be aware of it.

The first week of June I rode my orange Harley over to Napoleon Road and headed east out on route six bound for the turnpike to Cleveland. High school was over, eight years of foster care was over, and I felt strangely free, but freedom without a future is a dangerous place to be. And then there was always the issue of not realizing our sibling dream of getting back together. But, I figured I would be spending the summer with my brother, and we had a lot of catching up to do. I just hoped it wasn't too late to forge some of the emotional ties I hoped were still there. Neither one of us talked about Lee. I think we both just thought she had taken some irreversible steps that we were simply not privy to yet. After all, she was a very smart girl.

About the end of July, my friend's mom got tired of me living at the house and asked me to leave. I decided to go out to live with my brother in his refurbished barn east of town. That same week I also decided to sell my motorcycle. It had been starting to use oil, and it was time to sell it or put money in it. I got more money than I had in it so it was a good decision for me. That weekend my brother and I drove down to Bowling Green to see a high school friend of mine about buying a car. He had an old VW Karman-Ghia in his garage that his deceased dad had left him. He was tired of looking at it and didn't want to go to the expense of fixing it, so he just signed the title over to me. My brother and I towed the car out to my old foster parent's house and, after a few hours, got it running well enough to begin the trip back to Cleveland. A trip that should have lasted just over two hours took over six. We had to stop every ten miles or less to add oil and let the engine cool down. By the time we got into Chagrin Falls, the engine was so hot it was nearly on fire. Geoff ran every red light and every stop sign getting through the town-square out to the barn before the car incinerated. Fortunately he made it, and in a few days I had a drivable car with a good used engine in it—thanks to my mechanically minded brother.

With my motorcycle gone and a good car in hand, I began to rethink my original plan of driving around the country like Easy Rider. Geoff had an old high school friend who wanted to go to Minneapolis and start a rock band. Geoff had told him I could sing, so he asked me one night if I was interested. My brother told me that he might be interested in going with me to work on his pottery career, so that was a real enticement to the offer. So, about the time many of my friends were headed off to college in late August, I was headed to Minneapolis, Minnesota, to become the lead singer in a new rock-band venture. Unfortunately, those bright lights of the Aurora Borealis we witnessed on the way to the Twin Cities would soon turn to a much darker shade before this stage of my life would be over, but it was an inevitable phase through which I needed to pass. Yet on that crisp, clear night on the freeway through Wisconsin, I thought I might be entering the Nirvana stage of my young, purposeless life.

We finally got into Minneapolis about 9:30 in the morning the last Saturday of the month before Labor Day and called our friends Paul and his girlfriend. They had already arrived a few days earlier and had begun looking for a house to rent. They suggested we meet them for breakfast in Dinkytown, a college suburb of Minneapolis. Right after breakfast, we went out just over the railroad trestle to look at a couple of houses on the streets by the park. By noon we had seen about three houses in the area and decided on a big old three-story on 13th avenue. It had several bedrooms and, before the day was over, we had all picked out a room and begun putting our stuff in it. With four of us sharing the rent, I easily paid my first month's payment with the profit from selling my bike. We all celebrated our new home by smoking dope in the living room and talking about the prospects of finding key band members. Paul was a bass player, and I would sing lead, but we needed a lead guitarist and a good drummer for starters. For the next few weeks, Paul and I began to answer ads for guitarists and drummers.

The search took us all over the Twin Cities, and we met some very interesting people. One afternoon we met a lead guitarist whom we thought might be who we were looking for. His wife worked for the telephone company and made good money, so he didn't have to hold a day job. He was a little older than we were, but his ambition was to play steady in a band, just like us. He had been in a few but had never been in a position to go anywhere with it. As we listened to him audition that afternoon, we were blown away by his skill at playing long, intense riffs. We decided to get together the next day. The next morning Paul and I went down to a band supply store in Minneapolis to find some sound equipment. I bought a nice amplifier, some speakers and a mike for myself. We went back to the house and set everything up in an attic room which is where we would practice for the next five months. We went through a few drummers in the process, but finally got a decent local drummer from town. His dad had money, and he usually showed up for practice with a nice car, and he had a nice set of drums to boot.

My brother wasn't interested in the band, but it was still good to have him there in the same house. It was hard to know exactly why he had decided to come with me on this venture. He certainly wasn't ready to settle down or anything, but I guess he might have just been looking for a change. He wasn't doing anything in Chagrin, and he probably thought that it was a good opportunity to see a different part of the country. He began to set up a pottery studio in the basement and look around the area for clay supplies and a wheel on which to throw some pots. On the weekends, we would visit the bars together and get drunk. Neither of us talked about our sister. I think we both realized at this point, it was simply speculation as to where she had gone. We were satisfied in silently waiting it out. The bottom line was that she would show up when she was ready, and we would have the time we both desired to catch up on the years.

It was just after Halloween when Geoff gave me the surprising news that he was heading back to Chagrin Falls. He offhandedly said there really wasn't much for him in Minneapolis, and I think he was missing an old girl friend. He asked me to take him down to the interstate where he could start hitchhiking back to northeast Ohio. Late afternoon in early November, I dropped him off near the interstate. He let me know about a week later that he had gotten back no worse for the wear. With my brother gone, there was now nothing to do but jam with the band during the day and carouse at night. I also got a job just before Christmas delivering pharmaceuticals around the Twin Cities in an old delivery truck. I didn't make much, but I didn't need that much to live. Two girls which I knew from the restaurant in Dinkytown would feed me at least three or four times a week on the house, and I bought food and brought it home to cook on occasion. When we weren't practicing as a band, we were usually smoking dope, drinking, or both.

Just after the New Year, we started sending out some demo tapes to some local bars who provided live music. Our first gig was in the seediest section of Minneapolis at a sort of blues bar. We played that night and then used that occasion as leverage on another gig nearby. This went on for a few weeks, but it was going to take awhile for us to move up. I remember that while we were playing in the worst part of Minneapolis, a band by the name of Cheap Trick was playing at the largest venues in town. We figured if they could do that with a three man band, we could do it with four of us, but breaks or good fortune did not seem to be on our horizon.

In late January on an off night, I went down into town to drink and carouse at a place called Moby Dick's. It wasn't the nicest place in town, but it was crowded, and there were some pool tables. I played some pool and drank several rum and cokes until about 11:30 or so. The front of the place had several pinball machines in front which were usually quite popular until about this time, so I was leaning on one of the machines when I finished my drink. I must have been a little frustrated at my lack of success in finding female companionship, so I decided to tip my hat by breaking my glass on the end of the pinball machine before exiting the front door. I was clearly intoxicated and in no condition for someone to make trouble about it. Unfortunately, the bouncer, who was twice my size, decided that I needed both some trouble and some help out the door. As I went to leave, I felt a heavy blow against my head knocking me out the door and onto the concrete just outside. I simply had no idea that a bouncer might have taken offense at my careless destruction of property and lack of concern for other patrons inside the bar. I had hardly gotten back to my feet when I was met with another fist to my face. This time I realized what was happening, but I had little control over it. That punch nearly caused me to lose consciousness. Somehow, I managed to stand back up to face whoever it was who was hitting me, only to realize that I was facing the bouncer I had barely noticed inside. Addressing me with very profane terms, he hit me two or three more times before I could react. The last time he slipped to his knees while swinging and I saw this as my only chance to fight back. I too was on my knees and I grabbed his shirt with my left hand and tried to punch him with my right hand. Unfortunately, I was too drunk to fight, and all I ended up with was a handful of his new silk shirt. Infuriated at destroying his shirt, he jumped to his feet and began to kick me with his boots. Somewhere around five kicks, I passed out with a kick to my head. I don't know how many more times he kicked me after I was out.

Several minutes later, I came to and slowly climbed to my feet. There were a few people standing nearby who I could hear talking about the beating, but they said nothing to me or offered any help. I staggered down the street for a few minutes until I came to my senses. Then I began to realize that I was badly injured. I found a cab around the corner and had the driver take me back to the house in Dinkytown. When I stumbled in the door, my bass player said I looked like something out of a dirty Harry movie. In a few minutes we were on our way to the hospital in his truck. When I looked in the mirror I realized he was probably right about going. In less than an hour I was admitted to the General Hospital with hematomas in both eyes, a broken nose, a fractured skull, and three broken ribs. Fortunately, after four days in a general ward bed, I was able to be released to go home.

Not long after getting home, the band continued to practice and play, but something had clearly changed for me. The beating had left me with little incentive to practice and learn lyrics. Not only that, but I had decided that physical revenge against the bouncer at Moby Dick's was out of the question, so I sought out the services of a lawyer in St. Paul to press charges against the establishment. I figured if I went to St. Paul there might be less possibility of a lawyer being pressured by unseen, local forces in Minneapolis. Unfortunately, none of that mattered. For some reason, after taking extensive pictures of my yet visible wounds, and hearing my side of what happened, the lawyers called me to their offices in less than a week with a thumbs down on any law suit. Unfortunately, I didn't have the foresight, much less the ability to lock down witnesses the night it happened, and without them it was my word against Moby Dick's. Unless I wanted to go back with a gun or a baseball bat, I would have to leave it there, and now that I had sought out legal help, there would be significantly more incentive to walk away, so that's what I did.

We had another gig in town sometime in late February, but I had for all intents and purposes already checked out. We finished after two nights because I had lost my voice, and we couldn't fulfill the contract. In less than two weeks, I told the guys that I wasn't interested in continuing and had decided to head back to Ohio. I bought an old 1958 Plymouth station wagon from Paul, the bass player, and began to pack it up for the move east. He had won it in some raffle back in the previous fall and decided it wasn't worth keeping. I had sold my VW Ghia in November just after Geoff had left. The engine was damaged, and I couldn't afford to repair it, so the Plymouth became my only choice for transportation. Sometime around the second week of March, I was on my way back to Ohio.

In some ways, it was good to be headed back to more familiar surroundings. Little had changed in the year after high school, and there still seemed to be some possibility for happiness in my future. Spring was in the air, and as I wound my way through Chicago I was hopeful too that I might soon hear from Lee. Silence on that front was probably a good thing if that's what she needed, but my brother and I wanted to hear from her, and a fresh, new season renewed my hopes. Maybe someone had heard something in Bowling Green during the past year that would be encouraging to both of us. I could only hope.

I decided I would drive to my old foster home at Dan and Carol's to stay at least for the foreseeable future. My old upstairs bedroom was still available, and for the meantime my old house seemed welcoming. I would need to look for a job immediately and help with a few expenses, but not much else was important at the time. I decided to look close to home for a job, and I landed one in the lumberyard of a nearby building materials company which was about three miles from my house. It wasn't much of a job, but it kept me busy during the day, and provided beer and dope money. We would unload rail cars of lumber products, service the customers, and keep the premises clean for business. A day didn't go by that I didn't think I would finally get some personal news from Lee. Nobody around town knew anything more than I did, so it was simply a matter of waiting. Eric was to be released from prison in a month or so, and not knowing they had actually divorced, I wondered how their marriage was at this point, and more importantly, whether that would bring Lee out of her self-imposed vanishing act.

The first week of April was a busy month at work. People were in the remodeling mode, and we were running orders like crazy. Early one afternoon, I noticed Carol walking back through the yard toward me. I could tell that something was wrong by the look on her face, and she pulled me aside by the main building. Other than a tragedy in her family, I couldn't figure out what else could have induced her to seek me out at work. But once I saw her expression up close, I recognized the twin emotions of despair and sympathy. It was the latter in her eyes that made me realize it wasn't her family, it was mine. She said, "Bruce, I'm so sorry to have to tell you this, but Michigan State Police have discovered the remains of two women in southern Michigan and have identified one of them as your sister. She was murdered about a year ago. It was aired on TV last night as probable, but they confirmed it today. They didn't know where to find you to let you know, and I just got the call."

For the first time in just over eight years since that day in Waterville, I now had an official answer to the hope of my adolescence and the incessant dream of reclaiming my family. The answer came like a freight train into my heart, and for a moment I was overwhelmed, then I was confused, and then I was angry, and then silent. Carol asked me if I was all right. I shook my head yes, and then blurted out, "How did it happen?" She answered, "They're questioning a guy in Houston who is a serial killer from Michigan, but they're not sure yet. Do you want to go home? Your boss said you could take the rest of the day off if you want." I replied, "No. I'll finish the day and see you later. I think I need something to do right now, but thanks for asking." She stood there momentarily as I turned to walk back toward the loading barn, and then, reluctantly, she walked back out to her car.

I knew Carol was hurting for me, but she was hurting too. Our families went all the way back to where my childhood memories began. She rode our bus when we were on the farm with dad. She, just a year older than Lee, had spent many a day on our farm during the summer months between school years. Nothing had turned out the way either of us had imagined.

Piecing together Lee's final days is not an easy task. Her last parole check-in was on March 15th, 1974 — right about the time of my hockey championship in town. My brother and I came looking for her just five days later, but she was already gone. She and her girlfriend Debbie had met Gary Taylor in a bar on East Broadway in Toledo. Gary introduced himself as a Detroit auto executive looking for a good time. Actually, he was an escapee from the State Forensic Center in Ypsilanti, Michigan since 1973. He had been in and out of Psychiatric care and prison for over fourteen years and according to his own admission, had a "compulsion to hurt women." Sometime around the last week of March, Lee and Debbie followed Gary Taylor to a location south of Onstead, Michigan where he owned a home with his estranged wife, Helen who lived in Houston, Texas. After arriving at the house, Taylor evidently herded my sister and her girlfriend into the basement where according to FBI records, white slavery had been practiced. I have never examined the FBI report but the mayhem and torture practiced upon my loved one and her friend was simply unutterable horror. He finally ended their lives with a gun. Debbie was shot between the eyes and in her chin. Lee evidently died with a single bullet behind her ear.

My mind was reeling as the reality of death began to bear down on me. I thought of that day Geoff and I drove up to Toledo looking for her at the bar apartment where she stayed. We were just a few days late and didn't know where she might have gone. Now I knew, but that didn't help. I thought of Geoff, and that I needed to tell him. If the authorities hadn't been able to find me, I knew they wouldn't be able to find him. After work, I went home and called Mike, a friend of mine who was Geoff's age to tell him about Lee, and predictably, he had already heard. He asked me if he could lend a hand in any way, and I thought it might help if he would go with me to Cleveland to give my brother the news. He said he had some things to do until about nine o'clock that night, but we could leave about then. We finally got into Chagrin Falls about one in the morning and we went to where I thought Geoff would be, out at his old barn. He wasn't there and so we went up to the bar near the Popcorn Shop to see if anybody knew where he was or had seen him. Actually, I hadn't seen him since I got back from the Twin Cities. It had been almost five months.

Finally about four in the morning we found him in a rented house and had to get him out of bed. Walking out to find us in the side yard at four in the morning was all Geoff needed to know this wasn't a planned visit. I told him the news, but I think he had already guessed why I was there. We all decided to go get some breakfast somewhere and, on the way, I gave Geoff the newspaper clipping I had brought with me from the local Bowling Green paper. He read it slowly and deliberately.

Closure is a strange thing. You think you need it, but when it does finally arrive, it still knocks the air out of you. I was called to the Cleveland Clinic the night my birth mother died in 2000, and despite the lack of reciprocity between us, I wept when I had to honor her no-resuscitation order. Despite her original intention to abort me, she was my mother after all.

For both Geoff and me, it was the end of more than our sister's life. It was now the end of a hope for which we had long waited. That was the hard part. What good is family if it's not together? What good is love if you can't share it? That hope is what had gotten us out of bed in the morning for several years, and I don't think either one of us had a Plan B. I know I didn't, and I was beginning to get depressed. Geoff's spirits were down too, but neither one of us really had the capacity to console one another.

We left the 24-hour diner about five thirty in the morning and decided to drive out to a state park in the area. It had a lot of walking trails and some elevated ones, which kind of wrapped around the river. The higher walking trail was on a ridge and was probably a hundred seventy-five feet above the river on a very steep and jagged incline. After entering the walkway from the stairs, we all began to walk down the wide path just after the sun was coming up. I had hardly noticed the dawn, when for some reason I decided to sit down to try and sort out my thoughts while Geoff and Mike walked on ahead. During the whole drive up to Chagrin I had done some thinking about the last eight years. It had been one foster home after another. I never liked any of them, and I never loved the parents. I wouldn't let myself.

I had thought that if I gave away my love to them, I would be giving them what I was saving for my family. They were all I ever wanted, and I was now forced to admit that it would never happen. The long-held hope of my youth was officially over, and I couldn't come to grips with it. Hope gives meaning to life, and without it, life loses its directional signals. Slowly, I felt my grief begin turning to depression, and for the first time my inner resolve was cracking. Sitting down on a flat rock, which had obviously been a seat to many other passersby, I looked for a moment down at the river rushing through the ravine. I don't know how long I sat there but at some point, I felt a hand on my shoulder. Thinking Geoff had doubled back to be with me, I just kept watching the torrent of water down below and almost immediately with that thought, I felt the urge to hurl myself over the rock ledge. Had I done it, it would have meant almost certain death. As that thought came, I instantly turned around to speak to Geoff, but Geoff was not there.

He had not been behind me at all. During these last few minutes, both Geoff and Mike were a few hundred yards ahead. Then I suddenly felt the urge to jump again, with verbal encouragements coming from nowhere to end it now. With the hair literally standing up on the back of my neck, I jumped up to my feet and walked down the path toward my brother and Mike. As I walked, the presence left me, and I felt alone again. Whatever it was, it was now gone. As I approached the other guys, I saw that they were standing in front of a huge rock, which looked like it had fallen down from above the path long ago. It had lodged itself on a large flat area just off the side of the walking path. They were standing there apparently mesmerized by the image, which had been inscribed on the rock face by local Indians decades earlier.

It was some sort of portrayal of the Indian's view of the life cycle. Its ultimate message appeared to be that life was eternal, but at the same time it seemed like it was life from a dark, hellish source. When I looked over at my older brother his eyes were as big as saucers, and it was obvious that he had been affected by the same presence I had just felt back on the ledge. Mike had a similar look on his face and without saying anything we all turned and just continued walking down the trail. Shortly after, we ended up back on a walkway that led to where the car was parked. By the time we got back in the car, the sun was completely out, and it had warmed up considerably. None of us talked any further about our mutual experiences up on the trail.

We decided to head back to the house where Geoff was staying when an old high school friend of his pulled up to say hi. He had an old Plymouth convertible and after finding out what was going on, offered to spend the day driving us around in his car. None of us had a plan, so it sounded good to us. In a few minutes we were in the country riding around the back roads. It was kind of weird; I don't think any of us would have ever planned to be together at a time like this, but there we were— united in death. Death is the great equalizer. It brings people together on the worst of occasions.

Everything of that day seems a blur now, but I had another unforgettable moment in the backseat of that old convertible. I don't know where we were, and at the time I didn't much care, but Pete the driver had turned on the radio. It was blaring out one song after another when I began to think about what I had experienced back at the park ravine. I was beginning to focus on my depressive thoughts again when one of my then favorite songs came on—*Stairway to Heaven* by Led Zeppelin. As I listened, I now began to think about whether I would ever see either my dad or sister again. I knew they were somewhere, but I didn't have any idea where. Perhaps this song could help me I thought. Could lead singer

Plant or guitarist Page offer some timely insights into what was on the other side, should there be one? I had listened to the song scores of times before that, but that day, the song seemed to repeat things in my head that I was presently struggling with. So much of life to this point had seemed unkind.

I was tired, and I thought my internal struggle was reaching a breaking point. I couldn't help but think that perhaps it was time to give in to the pressure. I didn't have much left to resist anyway. At this point, I heard the lyric again,

Yes there are two paths you can go by. But in the long run.
There's still time to change the road you're on.
Your head is humming and it won't go — in case you don't know.
The piper's calling you to join him.

At that moment I felt another urge similar to the one I felt on the path. But this time it wasn't about throwing myself over a ravine. It was another voice, suggesting I give up my will and stop resisting internal restraints. Somehow I knew that to do it meant turning my back on everything I had ever known that was right. It seemed like it was the ultimate act of rebellion, which previously I had only dabbled at in my unruly life. This was different. This was an overture, which called for my total compliance. But for some reason, the urge passed, the song changed, and in a few minutes we were all talking about getting something to eat. I don't think I ever gave it much thought after that day, but I was aware that whatever it was, it wasn't simply harmless imagination.

By the time Mike and I said goodbye to Geoff and headed back home that night we were both physically and emotionally weary. That is always a prescription for wrong thinking and something had changed for me in those hours. I had already lived on the edge for a few years, but now any fear of the edge was even more diminished. I didn't know it at the time, but my greatest problem was the lack of hope. I had nothing to replace the hope of a reunited family. Now the road to the future seemed directionless and long. I went back to work on Monday at the lumberyard with little more incentive than just earning a paycheck. About the middle of the week, my sister's in-laws called me to ask about doing a memorial service the following week. Eric would be home from prison in time to attend, and they said it would be held in their church auditorium. I remember telling them that would be fine, and I would call Geoff to let him know.

By the next week, my grief had just begun to abate when it was now time to finalize the events of the past few days with an official memorial service. Geoff had gotten into town around the middle of the week and had driven over to Eric's parent's house. About ten-thirty in the morning, they both came out to pick me up in the country for the service all the way across town. The auditorium was nearly filled that morning when the pastor began the memorial service for Lee. I don't remember much about it, it was probably a bit liturgical with little real meaning to me, perhaps more for others, but from my perspective, it wasn't helpful.

When the service was over, Mrs. Hanneford took me aside and told me she wanted me to accompany her to the cemetery with Lee's cremated remains. I don't know why, but neither Geoff nor Eric wanted to come, so it was just she and I. For some reason, I felt comfortable with her. She had known our family for years, had known about my stepmother, about our having been orphaned, and at the time she seemed almost motherly to me. In reality, she was one of the few people in our town who knew all about what really had happened to our family.

We drove over to Oak Grove Cemetery and slowly wound our way around the area until we saw our family plot. She stopped the car, got out and walked over a short distance to my dad's grave marker. Unexpectedly, Mrs. Hanneford handed me a short-handled spade and told me she had gotten permission to put Lee's urn in the ground in front of my Dad's gravestone. She knew I had no money to buy a plot or erect a proper stone. Slowly, I centered the shovel about four or five feet directly in front of the marker and began to dig a few shovels full of sod and dirt. She handed me the cremation vase, and I unceremoniously placed it in the center of the hole I had made. I had done similar burials over the years, burying a frog, a dog, or a cat, but then I felt the weight of what was happening—I was burying my own sister. I was instantly overwhelmed. If I had not already let go of the hope of reuniting my family, I did then. Temporarily lost in thought, I forgot about Mrs. Hanneford.

Suddenly, I was in the kitchen on the farm. Lee and I were doing the dishes. She was washing. I was drying. We were singing "Pretty Woman" at the top of our lungs, and she was laughing at me for being such a little idiot. There I was feeling the warmth of the family kitchen, and the security of home...

"Bruce, are you ready to go now?" Mrs. Hanneford asked.

Pulling myself back from my fantasy world, I just nodded and got up and slowly turned to walk back to the car. We were finished.

Nothing would ever be the same again. The emptiness was now greater than ever, and with that, I made an even larger effort at filling the void. I was often uptown at the bar or with friends doing dope. I had a few friends who were into cocaine, and we got together whenever our money and drug supplies coincided. In Cleveland the previous summer, I had injected the drug, but we spent that spring and early summer regularly snorting cheap coke a few nights a week. Around the first of May, about five or six friends of mine were driving around in my '58 Dodge station wagon. I was behind the wheel when we passed a cop going the opposite direction. He noticed that I wasn't staying in my lane, flipped around and pulled us over just in front of my old elementary school on Main St. I was arrested for driving drunk and spent the night in the city jail. Two weeks later, I lost my license and was sentenced to three days in the county jail. Because I couldn't drive, my job at the lumberyard was over.

By the end of May I started doing small jobs for spending money. I went to work for a guy doing farm work. Life was unraveling. Then Ron, one of my high school friends, sensing I needed some help, asked me if I was interested in sharing an apartment in town. So I packed up my things from Dan and Carol's and moved to a small apartment on Second St. The apartment house was owned by Mike's dad, the one who drove me to Chagrin Falls to give my brother the news of Lee's death.

Ron and I shared the expenses of the small, two-bedroom place. It was cheap living, and between the two of us, we could live and party as much as we wanted. His dad had also died when he was a young teen leaving him a small inheritance. He had just gotten the bulk of it and had bought a brand new Grand Prix. We both decided that at the end of the summer, we would pack up his new car and drive out to California to go to work for his uncle who owned a construction business. The prospect of that left me with a plan for later but little regard for the present. The month of June was a blur. Life in the fast lane had taken on new proportions of drug binges, heavy drinking, and all that went with it. I was going nowhere fast, and I wondered if I would make it to California by the time fall rolled around.

CHAPTER NINE

Changing the Leopard's Spots

GROWING UP IN my doctor father's home was not at all a religious experience in the real sense of the word. Dad, being an agnostic, had little regard if any for what we might call organized religion. It's funny, but, in retrospect, he should not have had a negative view of faith or Christian values. His grandfather was a Mennonite farmer preacher who had been a faithful minister in his life, and his own dad had strong moral values. Unfortunately, moral values and teaching are only a generation away from extinction no matter how strong or weak they might be. For some reason, my dad's choleric personality wasn't friendly to the dictates of anybody, even if in this case, it might be God. He lived his life like he was never going to die, and did all of the stuff that we now know today kills you. He was a heavy smoker, a hard drinker, slept little, and pushed all the boundaries of life. At his favorite watering holes after leaving the hospital, he was known for his improvisational jazz piano playing and partying with the patrons. He was also a notorious womanizer, often bringing his young nursing assistants home to the farm to enjoy our family and whatever else he provided. As a five or six year-old, I had no idea that these wonderful people I often would swim with in our pool were actually helping create the marital tensions we observed from the kitchen table as kids.

Had my dad lived beyond the years allotted him, there is a strong possibility that I would have taken on a very similar demeanor. It was an inevitable outcome, one that would have been impossible for me to change myself.

By the time I had been in my third foster home, I had been introduced to church life unlike anything I had ever known in my father's house. On May 14, 1967, I got up after the service in the Church of Christ, in Wayne, Ohio, and walked down the aisle of the church at the invitation of the pastor to be baptized. In a moment, I was telling the pastor that I wanted to be immersed so I could go to heaven. He quickly gave me instructions on where to go to change clothes and get ready. In a few minutes I was standing with him in the baptismal tank just behind the main platform. He baptized me in the name of the Father, the Son, and the Holy Spirit, and, coming up out of the water, I remember looking out at the packed auditorium full of farmers and kids with whom I went to school. One face that I will never forget was the look of the woman who played the organ. She had this huge smile on her face, and I couldn't help but think that my decision to come that morning had delighted her beyond words.

Unfortunately, my decision to be baptized extended

no further than the water and the words. I had gone down a dry sinner and come up a wet one. Absolutely nothing had been altered in either my mind or my heart. It was just one of those things that you do when you're too young to know what you're doing. I guess I wanted something that morning, but whatever I thought I wanted, it didn't work any magic then or later.

Now as July rolled around in 1975, I was without a car, a steady job, or little more than day-to-day money to get high. That was about the extent of both my ambition and my religion in which I had come to believe. I didn't think it at the time, but I was at the end of the line. I was nineteen, empty, unhappy, angry, and going nowhere. Something had to change for better or worse.

The fourth of July happened to fall on Friday that year in 1975. I spent most of the day working on my friend's farm baling and fixing fences. I got off in the early afternoon, and he took me back to my apartment. I showered and got ready to go out and find a party somewhere. Sometime before dark, already drunk and stoned, we stumbled over to the city park to watch the annual fireworks show. When it was over, we made the rounds to several parties, snorting dope and drinking. Sometime in the wee morning hours, someone dropped me off at my apartment, and I passed out in my own bed.

As Saturday morning dawned, I got up about ten o'clock to an empty residence. My roommate had not made it back yet, so I decided to walk up to the closest place I could think of to get something to eat. It turned out to be a burger joint four or five blocks from the apartment. I walked in about half past ten, ordered my food and sat down near a couple of guys I went to school with who motioned me over to where they were sitting. We were talking sporadically when I looked up and saw an old neighbor friend of mine sitting on the other side of the restaurant eating by himself. He happened to be the oldest son of the woman who got my mother riding horses before the divorce back on the farm. His family had lived just a few miles past our place, and all their kids rode the bus with us. He was the same age as my sister and had the same first name, Lee.

He hadn't noticed me, so I just watched him for a minute before getting up to go over to his table. There was something different about him that I couldn't put my finger on, and there was also something strangely arresting about his countenance. He seemed like there was a settled peace about him. I couldn't quite figure it out, but it was different. I had lived a lot longer than my nineteen years, and I knew there was something unique about this guy. As I finished and made my way over to dispose of my tray, I called him by name. We both immediately recognized each other, and I sat down in the chair directly across from him. In a few moments I asked him what had been going on in his life. With little hesitation, he told me that the previous December, he had been shipped out of Viet Nam.

When he got back into the U.S. and then back into town, he told me he stayed drunk for about a month. He said he simply didn't know how to cope with civilian life after seeing so many of his friends not make it back. He explained that one day his dad caught him at home while he was sober and took him down to meet his pastor in a city about thirty minutes away. Without elaborating, he told me that the pastor showed him what it meant to become a Christian, and he had become a believer in Jesus Christ. I had heard this before. One time in Minneapolis while we were getting high during band practice, a few guys from the Billy Graham Association knocked at our front door and asked me if I had ever become a believer in Jesus Christ. I told them I wasn't interested and shut the door in their faces. I would have never remembered that without having heard Lee's brief explanation. Then almost without hesitation, he asked me what I had been doing with my life. He knew about our broken home and my murdered sister, but he had never known much about me. During most of my high school years, he had been in basic training or in Viet Nam. I gave him a quick update, and basically told him that I wasn't doing anything important at the time, but I had plans to go out to California by summer's end. I then told him my observation about him across the room. I told him I noticed something about the way he appeared in his countenance.

Then again, without hesitation, he told he had some cassette tapes on the Bible, and wondered if I might be interested in hearing them for myself. I guess he picked up on my incredulity, adding that if I were interested he would come pick me up at my apartment in his beat-up, two-seater Jaguar in about thirty minutes. He said we could go out to his house and listen to them there. I wasn't really interested in hearing the tapes on the Bible, but I wanted to ride in his Jaguar, and see the old farm, so I told him I could be ready in thirty minutes.

In a few moments, we both left in different directions, and I began to walk back over to my apartment. The combination of seeing an old friend, being back in the country near my growing up place, along with the prospect of hearing a Christian presentation had me feeling a little weird, but I was sort of looking forward to spending some time with Lee. When I got back to the apartment, I saw one of my old apartment buddies standing out in the front yard. He had paid rent for a couple of weeks and then never showed up again. I hadn't seen him for a while, and I was actually surprised that he had shown up on a Saturday morning for apparently no reason. He asked me what I was up to, and I told him an old friend of mine was coming over to pick me in his Jaguar to go out in the country. I told him that he wanted me to hear some tapes about the Bible. Almost out of nowhere, he asked if he could join us. I told him that I didn't think that was a problem, but I forgot to tell him that it was only a two-seater car.

In a few minutes, Lee arrived, and when I told him we had another passenger, he just suggested that we listen to it in my apartment since we couldn't all get in the car. That really wasn't what I had been planning, but nevertheless, we headed inside. Momentarily, we all sat down in my tiny little apartment living room, while Lee gave us a little introduction to what we were about to hear. Just as he finished, and he was ready to turn the tape player on, there was a knock at my door. I didn't usually have visitors, but I quickly got up and answered the door only to see two of my high school acquaintances standing there asking me what I was doing for the day. I could only guess that they were there to drink beer or smoke dope, and I wasn't at all in the mood, so I told them that we were listening to a tape on the Bible with some guys. They were welcome to come in but that would be the extent of what was happening today.

To my surprise, they both said they weren't doing anything and would like to hear the tape, too. After a few minutes, we were all sitting down listening to a tape on the Biblical details regarding the second coming of Christ. The tape hadn't been running for more than a minute or so when there was another knock on my door. Lee turned the tape off, and once again I went to answer the knock. When I opened it I was not a little surprised to see three more acquaintances standing there asking me a similar question to the first two guys I had just let in. I told them what we were doing and that they were welcome to join us. I invited them to come in, they sat down, and after a few minutes of catching them up on what was going on, we once again turned the tape back on.

In a few minutes everyone in the room was engrossed in the most engaging exposition of the Bible any of us had likely ever encountered. The experienced speaker took us through a series of both Old Testament and New Testament scriptures, which detailed world conditions and then talked about the return of Christ. When the tape was over, you could have heard a pin drop across the street. The room was silent, like something had just sucked every ounce of air out of it.

After a few moments, I spoke up and asked Lee one very direct question: "Lee, I know what I have heard, and I want to know just one thing, what does it mean to actually be a Christian?" I could tell by the reaction of the others in the room that I was not the only one in the room who was wondering the same thing, but for whatever reason, no one else spoke up. Then Lee looked over at me and asked me if I wanted to know what he knew, and I simply nodded my head. Still no one said a word. In a moment Lee began to read verses to me from the New Testament book of Romans. He said he was going to take me down the *Roman's Road*. I had no idea what he was talking about. He then asked me if I knew what sin was. I told him I thought it was something like breaking the rules. He said, "Yea that's it, but it's really more than that. It's actually the breaking of God's laws, and the Bible says if we break one of them, we actually have broken all of them." He then read a verse from the *Roman's Road*. "For all have sinned, and come short of the glory of God." He then added another one nearby which sounded a lot like it: "For there is no one righteous, no not one."

For a moment, I let those words just rattle around in my head, but then I thought seriously about my life. It seemed pretty easy for me to accept that fact. I knew that if there was a God, and if he was in as much control of the world as these words inferred, then I was likely guilty of sin. I had not only sinned against my own conscience on too many occasions to count, I had also done some pretty nasty things to other people. I had arrived at the point in life where I hardly had any concern for others because I had become accustomed to the idea that no one really cared about me. I was almost to the point in my downward spiral as to not have any consideration for anybody, and I instinctively knew that this problem would only continue getting worse.

I looked back up at Lee and said, "I see that, keep going." He then read a verse to me that almost knocked me to the floor. He read the words out loud. You have to remember that Lee was talking to probably the least likely of all the people in the room to be receptive to any presentation about religion or Christianity. In fact, our conversation to this point was similar to one of those talk shows where an audience is listening in on a person's most sensitive life situations with bated breath. Everyone's eyes in the room were now riveted on me. I wasn't aware of it at the moment, although I felt as if I was almost like a group rep for everyone else's questions. I was, at least in my own mind, the only person in that cramped living room that morning. The second verse he read was, "But God commends his love toward us in that while we were yet sinners, Christ died for us."

For a moment, I didn't quite understand the point, but then I flipped the verse around in my mind and thought about it. Here I was searching for the last eight years for human love, family love, to fix my broken heart and empty life. The entire reason I wanted my family back was because I had convinced myself that it would bring back the warm security of the home and farm life my dad had provided. It hadn't happened, and now I knew that it wasn't ever going to happen. Perhaps, I thought, it wasn't even meant to happen. What if God had allowed everything over the last eight years to bring me to this single, solitary moment? The thought stunned me, but somehow it slowly began to make sense. I thought, if I have come through all of this without ending up in prison, dying prematurely, or committing suicide, perhaps there is something that God ultimately wanted me to know.

I couldn't get away from those words; "But God commends his love toward us, in that while we were yet sinners..." That was what was really shocking to me because it actually said that God loved us even now, including me. For a second I wanted to be incredulous in the face of God and ask, "If You loved me, why did You put me through all this pain without my family and then allow me to bury my own sister? Is that Your love?"

But after thinking that, I wondered if God could have allowed it to happen so that I might be willing to look for answers elsewhere. I couldn't quite come to grips with it. Then Lee, as if sensing my momentary confusion, took me to the next verse. It was from Romans 6:23, and he read it out loud just like the others: "The wages of sin is death." As he read that verse, I couldn't stop the impulse of remembering that afternoon at Oak Grove Cemetery where I had buried Lee's ashes. The day of the memorial service, it was just me and the funeral director from town. I can't forget the feeling of pulling up a big spade of dirt and sod and putting Lee's remains in the hole. All I could think at the time was that I was burying both my sister and the hope of getting my family back. But on this particular morning, I didn't think that thought. I thought of how Lee's life had actually dictated her death. Her Christian father-in-law had quoted a verse in the effort to put a face on Lee's untimely passing. From Hosea 8:7, he said that she "had sowed to the wind, and reaped a whirlwind."

Then I saw something alarming in that moment that startled me. I was on the same road my sister had been on and hadn't even realized it until that instant. She had, by the nature of her life choices, imperiled her own safety, and without knowing it, her very life. In the end, the wages or paycheck for sin is exactly that, death. Death by definition simply means separation. On the physical side of things, it is separation from the body, and everyone faces that prospect. On the spiritual side of things, it is separation from God. At that moment I couldn't help but feel like I was dangling over hell on a shoestring. Before I knew it, my Bible quoting friend read the rest of that verse, "But the gift of God is eternal life through Jesus Christ our Lord."

Have you ever been to the Grand Canyon and looked out over that enormous precipice and down into that huge hole which stretches at its widest point for eighteen miles to other side? I did that one bright, clear, spring morning for the first time. To say it is breathtaking doesn't quite describe it. I've been in a helicopter 2500 feet above Niagara Falls watching the river converge at Niagara and the tremendous foam and mist thundering up from its wake. It too, is equally awesome and overwhelming.

But those things pale in comparison to what that verse spoke to me that morning on July 5, 1975. If I was hearing things correctly, God had not only loved me all along my ugly broken road, but Jesus Christ, who had died for me, was in effect, offering me a free gift. It was a gift, which was rooted in his life offered for my sin on His cross. Somehow, I knew that I couldn't say no to this offer. In fact, I wanted this more than anything. It was now dead silent in my little living room. No one was speaking, and I didn't even know if anyone else was breathing at that moment.

My living room, which was usually just a place for getting stoned or for gratuitous sex, had now become an altar. All I remember is that I looked up at my friend and asked him what I would have to do to actually become a Christian. Expecting a long answer, I shifted my weight and waited for his reply. I can't forget it. He simply said, "Why don't you just pray." I said, "What do you mean, right now?" He said, "Yea, right now." So without even so much as a thought, I bowed my head in my own living room in the midst of several life-long acquaintances and began to word a very intimate and sincere prayer to God. The funniest part of this was that I actually prayed out loud! I don't remember the exact conversation. All I remember is telling God that I was thankful that Jesus died for my sin, and that nothing would keep me from trusting Him as the Savior. When I said, "Amen," I lifted my head and realized that something had taken place in those few intense moments. All of a sudden, my inward sense of shame and the weight of guilt that I had carried for so long were no longer there. I don't know how else to describe it, but I was not the same as I was just moments before.

I was so overwhelmed that I had to excuse myself from the room to walk outdoors through the sliding doors just to my left. Out on the street I began slowly walking trying to collect my thoughts. I saw a little church on the next corner and decided to just slip in for a few moments of silence by myself.

When I went in the door, there were no lights on, but I could see well enough to walk down to the altar, and so I knelt down to pray. Once again, I remember only trying to thank God for what had just happened in my living room a moment before. Then I got up and saw this lighted framed picture of Jesus on the far wall of the little sanctuary. I easily recognized the picture, having seen it on several occasions in other churches, so I walked over to it. I was drawn to Christ's serene gaze up toward heaven, and I just stood there for several minutes talking to the picture. Yes, if the janitor was watching me that morning from the hallway, he must have been chuckling at the crackpot talking to Jesus!

I don't know how long I stood there in my one-way conversation, but I finally walked back to the apartment to find that two other guys had also believed in a similar fashion as I had. I didn't get a chance to talk to them, but it had been quite the chance meeting for several of us that morning, especially for someone who almost never had visitors. As the living room emptied out Lee stayed for a few minutes longer and we talked. We made plans to go to his dad's church the following Sunday and then almost as quickly as he came, he left to head back out into the country.

I didn't have any plans the rest of the day, but a few hours later Eric came over to my apartment and asked me if I wanted to go get a few beers with him later in the evening. He had only been out of prison for a few months at this time and had found a job in construction across town. We decided to meet at his house, and we walked to the bar from there. Somewhere along the way, I announced to him that I had become a Christian that morning. I'm not exactly sure of his response, but surprisingly he didn't laugh or think it was a joke. Actually, I think he was surprised. Eric was one of the toughest individuals I ever met in my life. I remember years earlier, one night before he was arrested he asked me if I wanted to learn how to box out in his garage. I didn't know it, but many other foolish people had taken him up on that offer before. I was fifteen, strong, fast, and just not smart enough to say no to an ex-golden gloves fighter. At the time he was no more than a hundred-twenty pound junkie. But, just moments after he got me all heated up in a quick boxing tutorial, I was sent flying across the garage with a punch I never even saw coming. When I came to from my crumpled position on the floor over against the garage door, I looked up to see him standing over me laughing out loud.

We walked into the bar that evening, got a table, turned on the jukebox, and ordered a couple pitchers of beer. In a few minutes, we were joined by some girls and a few other friends also joined us. I don't think we had been there for over thirty minutes before I started feeling like a fish out of water. I couldn't understand what had come over me, but for some reason, unknown to me, everything in that bar made me sick. The lights, the music, the people, the talk, the environment, everything seemed to be at odds with me. I sat there and listened to conversation, and tried to act normally, but normal was somehow not normal anymore. Finally, my discomfort got so intense I had to excuse myself to go to the men's room. When I came back to the table, Eric had gotten up to dance with one of the girls, so I just left. Stepping outside into the hot July night, I began to walk back up Main Street the twenty blocks or so to my apartment. It was a long walk, and it gave me time to really think through what it was that I was experiencing. I'm not sure I figured it out that night, but somehow I recognized that life was no longer going to be the same. In some strange way I was beginning to actually detest the life to which I had been so long accustomed. I didn't want it anymore, but at this point, I didn't really know what I wanted. One thing was certain though. Something was different, and I was determined to find out what exactly that meant.

A week later, Lee called me to ask if I was interested in attending a church where his dad attended south of Bowling Green. For the past week I had done nothing but work and then come home and voraciously read my old Bible, which had been given me in one of my foster homes. The idea of meeting a bunch of other Christians seemed like a great idea, and all of a sudden Sunday morning church took on a whole new persona. After church, I spoke with the pastor about being baptized, and he made arrangements for the next Sunday, right after the morning service.

We returned the next Sunday, and right after the baptismal service some older gentleman wanted both Lee and I at the back of the auditorium. After I got dressed I joined Lee and this other man, who turned out to be a pastor from a nearby community. He told us that he was seriously considering starting a new church in our town and asked if we would be willing to help launch it by summer's end. Actually, I don't think we could have been more enthusiastic about it. Not only was it a great opportunity to get in on the ground floor of a new church, we wouldn't have to drive sixty miles round trip anymore for worship services.

CHAPTER TEN

How Do You Forgive?

BY THE END of August, we began the new church with Pastor Lloyd, and my new-found Christian life took on a whole new perspective. As a new believer, I guess I was pretty lucky in some ways. For many people who become believers, their Christian life is not as extreme as it was for me. They may have been morally upright and honest people, with strong moral values, having been raised in respectable homes before their conversions. That wasn't my background. I might have been raised in some respectable homes, and had been taught values, but none of it had stuck. I had, for some time, been walking the line between jail and an early grave, just like my sister Lee. It was simply a matter of how long and which one. Fortunately, I had been graciously spared from both.

It wasn't that I felt I had to go to church; it was that I wanted to go. I wanted to grow in my faith and find out where this new path might lead me. Pastor Lloyd's son-in-law happened to be the music director at the new church, and it wasn't long before he found out that I enjoyed singing. Almost immediately, he began to ask me to sing on Sunday nights at the service and join him in duets. For the first several months my Christian life blossomed. Several of my old acquaintances, once they discovered that I was a Christian, either stopped by my house or came to church to see what I was doing. Unfortunately, in a matter of months, I barely saw them anymore. Our paths had taken completely different directions.

I ended up several weeks after my conversion moving in with my friend Lee, who offered me a room at his house. His mother, my real mother's old friend who got her riding horses, often made us dinner or invited us over across the pond on their property for a get together. They lived about two miles east of my dad's old farmhouse and land. Oftentimes after Sunday dinner, I would take a walk down on the pastureland by the river which our family had once owned. I knew it all very well. I still recognized every turn and twist in the creek and just about every tree along the pastureland on the property that I had either climbed or had permanently etched on my adolescent memory. I remembered the fence line and many of the old posts, which marked the property I had carried or helped the hired hand put in the ground as a boy. As summer turned to the chilly fall days, my heart reeled with memories every Sunday afternoon as I walked and re-explored my old stomping grounds. The sights, the smells, and the feel of it brought back the contented days of my happiest years on earth. It became a Sunday after-church ritual for several months.

However, it was sometime in February or early March when I noticed something had happened to all my spiritual zest. Oh, I was still going to church, but it wasn't like it was before. In fact, I had begun to teach a small class on Sunday mornings, and I was still singing with Charles the worship leader, but my heart had grown cold for some reason. I started wondering about it, and one day after church I was taking my usual walk around our old property when it dawned on me what my problem might be. For the past several weeks, what once was enjoyable and exhilarating in my Sunday after-church stroll had become shear drudgery. I noticed that I had moved on from enjoying the old memories to using them to fuel a growing resentment toward my stepmother for having, with the help of a local lawyer, taken everything my dad had intended for my siblings and me. Now I noticed as I walked through the property, I was no longer counting my blessings, but counting the loss of an earthly inheritance. I had been growing bitter for several weeks now and hadn't even noticed the change in me until it had nearly devastated my Christian walk.

My stepmother still owned and rented out the second largest house on my dad's property. I had ridden the bus with the two girls who lived on the property. They knew my stepmother as their landlord, and every time I walked back out of the woods and up through their barnyard on one of my Sunday walks, I wondered what it would be like to meet my stepmother sitting in the driveway in her yellow Cadillac. Sometimes, I fantasized about my justification for beating her with my fists; all the while she lay bleeding on the ground begging me to stop. I wanted to ask her why she had taken away my childhood and thrown it away like so much garbage. Why, when she knew that I was being tossed around from home to home like a rag doll as an adolescent, didn't she intervene and give me the mother's love I so desperately wanted? Why had she never even come to my sister's funeral or offered any assistance in giving her a decent burial? Why had she secretly taken the inheritance which my father had left his three children to "share, and share alike" as he had prescribed in his will?

Almost at the same time, these horrible memories began to control my conscious thoughts, I had begun to read Biblical passages about forgiveness, particularly the sins which Christ had forgiven me for as a Christian. The only thing I really hadn't done before I was converted was take an innocent life. It probably wasn't far from my future without Christ. As I thought about forgiveness, I realized that I had to make a choice to forgive what my stepmother had done. It wasn't emotionally easy. I had made a cottage industry out of my resentment and hostility for many years, and now I had allowed it to invade the most sacred thing I ever knew. Growing up in strangers' homes and boys' schools, and the like, it was what got me out of bed every morning and motivated me to hope for better while I endured the worst.

I think what finally convinced me that I was wrong to feel the way I did was when I recognized, that in reality, I would have never likely become a believer in the first

place had it not been for the path that led me there.
Actually, if the truth be told, my stepmother's actions
had been used to steer me into God's plan for my life.
Now, don't misunderstand what I'm saying. There is not
one ounce of justification for my stepmother in terms of
what she did. Without God's fathomless knowledge of
these matters and omnipotent ability to work all things
together for good, nothing profitable could have resulted
from her selfish and sinful choices. But the day came
when I eventually saw everything from this eternal
perspective rather than the limited view from which I
had been operating for months. When that happened,
everything became clear. I had to accept the fact that I
had traded in my earthly inheritance for a heavenly one,
plain and simple. I had traded in a few thousand for an
eternal treasure. What right did I now have to continue
quibbling over fool's gold by comparison? I made the
choice to forgive my stepmother.

Just a few weeks after this momentous shift in my
spiritual disposition, I found myself sitting in church one
Sunday evening listening to a sermon from Pastor
Lloyd. His message was from Luke, chapter nine, where
Jesus "set His face to go to Jerusalem." In Luke's
gospel, this is the point where Christ consciously
determines the course, which ultimately leads him to his
sacrificial death on the cross. He knows exactly that
what He is doing will lead to His crucifixion, suffering,
and death, but He proceeds as a man on a deliberate
mission. In the Old Testament book of Isaiah, the pastor
made the direct comparison of this text with that of the
divine prophet who "set his face like a flint." The
resolution of Jesus in these two passages was incredible

to me. My heart, recently softened by my newly discovered forgiveness was now overwhelmed by the commitment to life purpose that Jesus demonstrated in His brief but eternally significant life.

After the service, I found myself weeping uncontrollably on the front pew. For some people this might not seem very significant, but for me it was the first time in over eight years that I had openly cried anywhere. There were thirty or forty people there that night, and they all ushered themselves by my pew asking me if everything was ok. All I could tell them was that I had never been better! In reality, that night was a monumental occasion for me. My tears were brought on by my decision to offer my life to God to use in a full-time Christian vocation. For several months I had been entertaining the idea of going back to college to study physical therapy. I wanted to be in the medical field like my dad. To me, that now seemed like second best. When I left church that night, I felt like I had been connected to something almost eternal in terms of my life's purpose.

Whatever it was, I now had a calling, and that called for a plan.

CHAPTER ELEVEN

Beauty From Brokenness

JUST A FEW weeks later in 1976 as the first signs of spring began to appear, I got a job working construction in Toledo, Ohio. I had been delivering pizza over the winter months by the university, and now with a break in the winter weather it was time to get a better paying job to take me through the summer. The guy who rented the Porter farm from my stepmother stopped at my house one afternoon and said he had a job in Toledo if I wanted one, and he even offered to pick me up every morning on his way. As it turned out, it was an entry-level job, but it was steady work. Some days, I would be nailing subfloor with a hammer and an apron full of nails, but on most days I was continuously feeding the union carpenters with wood supply. It was hard work, and after the guys found out I was a new Christian, they made it their job to give me a hard time of it. Fortunately, it never got physical or abusive, so I took it as an opportunity to simply get stronger in my faith. We had one guy on the crew who was a part-time minister who the guys really didn't like, and he was always using me as a sounding board for his complaints. I was never much help to him. I figured if he couldn't take a little razzing, he probably couldn't succeed in life. He ended up leaving after a few months.

Not long after I started working full time, I decided to have a conversation with my pastor about the possibility of full-time ministry preparation. He invited me out for dinner one night, and I used the opportunity to tell him that I wanted to pursue Christian ministry. I recall him saying that he was not surprised by my decision as he had been praying about that very thing with his wife for a few weeks. He said he would make some calls for me and get the ball rolling. By the middle of June, I had applied and been accepted at a Bible college in Missouri. I had few clothes, an old 1963 Chevy Biscayne, and very little money saved. After considering my circumstances, I decided to go see one of my dad's pathology colleagues at the pathology lab in Bowling Green one morning. Dr. Tanginki happened to be in the lab and took me into his office to talk for a few minutes. I told him I had decided on going into the ministry and needed some help. Fortunately, he was my stepmother's employer the year we moved away from the family farm, and was well aware of what she had done, and immediately asked me how he could help me. I will never forget that moment because he stood up from his desk and literally took off his own suit jacket to see if it would fit me; I refused it. After an enjoyable visit he told me to call him when I got to school, and he would take care of my first month's tuition and board. Like a true family friend, he kept his word after I arrived at college in late August, and fortunately within that month I had landed a job to help with monthly college expenses.

After that visit, it seemed that the rest of the summer weeks flew by, and before I knew it I was heading to college. I was a little surprised by a couple of things after I arrived on campus. The first was the fact that many of the students arrived in far better shape than I did. I had one pair of dress pants, one tie, one French-collared shirt, and one older sport jacket, not to mention that I was driving an old Chevy sedan that gave me away as a true Ohio farm boy. The second thing that surprised me was how polished several of the students appeared to be as I compared myself to them. One such student approached me on the sidewalk as I made my way to move into the freshman dorm. He introduced himself, and then went on to tell me that he was enrolled as a missions major who would be going to Bolivia, South America, as an evangelist upon the completion of his four-year program. He then brashly asked me what my plans would be. Unfortunately, I had no such grandiose plan, and I frankly said that I didn't know what I would be doing. I think I did tell him that I had decided on a missions major because I thought I might be interested in ministry outside of the continental United States. All the while I was thinking to myself how lame I must have been for not having all these decisions already made for my future.

About that time, we hit the freshman dorm, and we went our separate ways. As an introduction to my fellow college students, I was now well aware that I had some ground to make up if I intended to fit in to this highly polished student body. I got placed in a four-man room with just two other roommates, one from Texas and the other from Oklahoma. To my surprise, the Texas boy was a preacher's son who evidenced some pretty obvious issues from the day he arrived. He not only had a cigar-smoking and drinking habit, but he was also super aggressive. Unfortunately, he also suffered from epilepsy. I am not sure why he was admitted, but it soon became clear that he was not going to last long. One night after coming in late to the room, he decided he was going to try to see if he could dislodge me from my bunk directly above him. After two jostling kicks from below I kindly asked him to stop or else I would be coming down. A few moments later he kicked my bed again and as I jumped out my bed to deal with him, I could tell from the look on his face that he was having a grand-mal seizure. In those days, it was still believed that the tongue could be swallowed and needed to be kept out of a patient's tracheal path to avoid suffocation. Dutifully, and without thinking, I reached into his mouth to attempt to "save" him when he clamped down on my two fingers. I didn't lose my fingers, but a few days later I thankfully lost my Texas roommate.

About a week later we got two new guys. One was from Kansas, and the other was from Indiana. The Kansas kid was kind of strange. He almost never attended class, slept all the time, and just walked around the dorm in his thick, white, terry cloth robe. The older guy was quiet and seemed quite strange. He too, smoked cigars, and seemed to have a plethora of intense personal issues for which he wanted late night counseling from his roommates. My Oklahoma buddy, Barry, and I would trade off counseling sessions for Frank. One Saturday morning Frank asked me if I wanted a ride to the bank to cash a work check. En route, he popped the question about helping him sight-in his new lever-action Winchester rifle. I declined and asked him to just drop me back off at the school. I didn't think I wanted any part of helping Frank sight-in his new gun.

The next week, about Tuesday, our dorm leader Gary called us for a meeting in our dorm room just after lunch. After sitting us down, he told us to brace ourselves for some bad news. Neither Barry, our Kansas sleeper roommate nor I had a clue what might be coming. Gary then asked me when I had last seen Frank. I told him that I saw him on Saturday, and that he said he was going out to sight-in his new rifle once he had dropped me off. He then told us that Frank had actually driven directly to Indiana that Saturday. Apparently, he had something more in mind than just getting his rifle to shoot straight. He drove to the trailer park of his ex-wife, and when her new boyfriend answered the door, Frank shot him dead. By this time, I was beginning to wonder if I had chosen the wrong place to prepare for ministry. Just a week after that, my Kansas sleeper roommate got sent packing for failure to attend class, and it was now down to just Barry and me in our four-man room. Fortunately, that's the way it would stay for the rest of the school year.

Barry was nothing in the mold of my other oddball roommates. He had given up a career in naval aviation for Christian service, and I knew after hearing him tell his story of surrender to the ministry that he was as serious as I was about making preparation. Just after the departure of my last roommate, I was heading to class about the middle of October when I passed the door of the "Bolivian Evangelist" guy who duly impressed me my first day on campus. He was shining his shoes by a packed footlocker, so I stopped to say hi and ask him where he was going. He confidently replied, much like the first time I met him, that God had now called him into the military. Two things became instantly clear to me; that God got the blame for a lot of things He didn't author, and secondly, that I wasn't nearly as green around the gills as I once thought.

My freshman academic schedule was full, and I also decided to join a men's singing group that fall in 1976. The group had a ten-day trip, which included a stop across the border of Canada, and this is when I first began to consider the northland as a possible ministry location upon graduation. When I got back from that cross-country trip, I was in the cafeteria one day for lunch when one of the cafeteria leaders asked me for my name. I introduced myself, and then he asked me if I knew where I might be interested in doing ministry. Fresh off our recent singing trip I told him I had been thinking a lot about Canada. He said that was interesting to him, because his dad had been stationed with the Sir Wilfred Grenfell Mission in Newfoundland and Labrador, and that he had been praying for men to go there to start new churches on the island. My first question to him was, "Where is Newfoundland?" He laughed, told me, and then asked me if I would at least consider praying about that possibility. Then he told me he had a good contact for me in St. John's, the capital, if

I thought I was interested. Well, I was in the cafeteria almost every day, and nearly every time before I could walk back out, my Newfoundland friend would speak to me about this island in the North Atlantic 350 miles from the north-eastern tip of Maine. Before that year ended, I was convinced that Newfoundland was part of my destiny, and so I started paying close attention to it.

There was also something else I started paying close attention to that year. When I returned from Christmas break, on our first full day back, I read the announcement by the mailboxes that we had a group practice on the second floor of the Administration building at one o'clock sharp. I happened to be the first member there, only to find that our regular piano player had decided not to return for the spring semester. In his place was the sister of our group leader attempting to bang out the new music, which her brother had just recently handed her. Her name was Grace, and she was beautiful. She was considered "Miss Popular" on campus, well known because of her role as yearbook editor as well as the solos she sang at our church, not to mention the fact that she was the daughter of my favorite theology professor.

After getting over my surprise at seeing her taking the place of our male pianist, I innocently asked her what she might be doing playing for our men's group. She told me that her brother had sought and gained permission from the administration for her to be our new pianist. My reaction was mixed but communicated poorly. Being attracted to her, but not wanting to show my hand too soon, I simply reacted by informing her that she definitely needed to practice. I had previously heard of her prima donna status, being a professor's daughter. She also had a reputation of dating guys once before moving on to "greener pastures", and I decided I would let her know early on that I wasn't going to be on her list of has-beens. I think it worked, but unfortunately I think she instantly despised me for my rude comment. The semester was indeed off to a great start.

There was something else worth mentioning about that spring semester my freshman year. I had joined the singing group for a couple of reasons. First, I loved to sing, and so it was natural for me to find an outlet once I got to college. But the other reason wasn't so great. You see I had belonged to a small city church back home in Ohio. We averaged no more than thirty or forty people on Sunday mornings. I sang solos, duets with Charles, and even taught an adult Sunday school class toward the end of my first full year there. I got used to the small manageable structure, and so when I got to school I was shocked to see the size of the churches. I joined a church of over eight hundred members, and I simply wasn't yet accustomed to singing or speaking before really large crowds. Consequently I joined the choir where I could sing with a degree of anonymity, taught a small boy's class, and sang with our traveling college choral group. I was still uncomfortable and insecure with the large churches in which I was now serving, but that was about to change.

That first day back for choral practice in the Administration building, our director walked straight up to me and handed me a piece of music and told me that I would be singing it as a solo for the entire semester and while on tour. The song's title was "I Must Choose to Surrender." I swallowed hard and then realized that it was no coincidence. I immediately began to recognize my failure to face my fear before, but now the Lord was giving me a fresh opportunity to grow in grace, not to mention the fact that this also allowed me to practice my solo piece with our new piano player.

I guess we actually could blame God for that one.

As spring classes started back in January, I had another packed semester along with the March tour with our men's singing group, and I was looking forward to it. By the time the tour rolled around Grace, our new piano player was beginning to warm up to me in some ways. She was still keeping a healthy distance but at the same time letting me know she was interested in getting to know me better. Well, the tour if not anything else, was the perfect venue for doing just that. Not only this, but I was singing my solo nearly every night somewhere across the southwestern part of the country and rambling by day in a comfortable, diesel coach with our fun-loving group. By the time we got back on campus, Grace had decided that it was now safe to go out on a date and so began our courtship.

We would often wait to go out on Sunday nights after church, and our first date was at a place called Shotgun Sam's Pizza Parlor. As we shared a pizza one Sunday night, she asked me to tell her more about my background, and so for the next several minutes I told her my story. I wondered at the time if I was hurting my future dating chances by opening up to her with all of the sordid details, but she had asked and wanted to know. Predictably, she had almost an exact opposite background from me. She had grown up in a pastor's home, had been a model young woman, an honor student, and her dad was presently the most respected theology professor on our campus. I was sure they had envisioned a much different sort of young man to be interested in dating their prized younger daughter. But to my amazement, Grace's response to me was not what I expected. Through the dark past, she seemed to see God's hand in having delivered me from the disaster of a broken life. She seemed to instinctively understand that I wasn't who I once was. When I took her home that night, I could see that this was more than just a Sunday night pizza date, and I think she felt the same way too.

By the time the school year began to wind to a close, we were dating regularly, and I had developed a good relationship with her entire family. Her brother Dwight, the leader of the singing group, and I had become good friends and hung out a lot. Her younger brother David was also a freshman, and we saw one-another on campus almost daily. I could see a lot of similarities between her family and my early family on the farm. Family life deeply attracted me, and I enjoyed Grace's home. I was therefore very surprised to find out her dad had been hired to lead a college in the northeast, and the family was scheduled to move to New Hampshire by the end of May. Grace had decided to move with the family upon the hope of getting into a Boston music conservatory.

Dwight and I had co-rented a house just before the move, and I had landed a summer job installing concrete driveways which would start the second week in June. That gave me just enough time to help drive one of their moving trucks and figure out how I was going to continue dating Grace. This, I thought, was going to be a problem. By the time I had returned back to Missouri, I accepted the fact that our relationship would now be a long-distance one, and letter writing would have to suffice, at least for the immediate future. It had already occurred to me that I had the option of transferring my credits to the new college in the fall. I tentatively applied and simply left it at that.

Grace and I exchanged letters two or three times a week and talked on the phone only occasionally. But, I was beginning to realize that starting another school year in Missouri was likely not going to happen. With that in mind, I continued working through June and July, and then the first week in August my boss, without warning, told me I didn't have a job anymore. I was shocked, but that day when I got home I found an acceptance letter from the new college in New Hampshire sitting in my mailbox. Having already prayed about the possibility of transferring, I took this as the final indication that God was orchestrating this decision for me, and so I immediately started making plans to move north.

Within a week, I had packed up my stuff, closed my local bank account, and was ready to begin the drive to my new future. It's funny when you know something is absolutely right but others around you seem to be like boat anchors around your ankles. Grace's brother didn't want me to transfer, my assistant pastor didn't want me to transfer, and I got little real encouragement from my home church in Ohio. It wasn't that they were actually opposed to my going; it was just that they didn't seem to fully understand why I would need to pick up and change things when things appeared to be going so well. I learned early on that sometimes no one needs to know but you, because in the end, only you have to answer to God for your decisions. It may be nice when others around you appear to sense the same things you do when you decide to do them, but I learned that will not always be the case.

By the time I left Missouri around the middle of August, I was ready to begin the next chapter of life. A few things had changed over the past year. I had grown up a lot for one thing. There is a lot to be learned by watching others your own age make decisions both good and bad. I had watched the lives of a lot of those who I had thought were on top of the world at the start of my freshman year just completely wash out or simply give up what seemed to be so certain to them at the beginning. I also learned afresh that taking on new risks which challenged you were the keys to growth both personally and professionally. By the time I arrived in Nashua, New Hampshire, it seemed like my freshman year was ancient history, and I was ready to move forward with what God had for my future.

After arriving, I stayed a few days with Grace's family until I could find a room with one of the families interested in housing a poor college student. I ended up getting a room with an extremely poor, uneducated family in a small apartment building in the city. It wasn't much, and I had to share a room with their son and share a bathroom with the entire family. The one good side of it was that Mrs. Palmer was an extraordinary cook, and she seemed to delight in making me happy with her food. Grace and I began to date regularly and one fall day in 1977, I asked her to marry me. I had saved for about three months in order to buy her an engagement ring, and I didn't like to wait once I was sure of something. I had no doubt that God had brought us together so that day in Greeley Park was the most exciting beginning I had ever known in a human relationship. Grace was a perfect match and always brought out the best in me. She had been born and raised in Memphis. I always have told her, partly in jest, that I wanted to marry "up" and had to go south to find a good wife.

We planned on an early June wedding as soon as the school year was behind us. That's just how it happened and when we returned from a Niagara Falls honeymoon, we settled into our little two-bedroom apartment on Amherst Street. As most young couples find out, going to school, working a full-time job, and beginning a brand new marriage is not the easiest thing in the world. We struggled along and felt like God was teaching us to learn to trust Him with our every need, no matter how great or small. I'll never forget the afternoon we were driving our one and only car into town late that first summer when I noticed while we were stopped at a light our car continued to bounce up and down. It was like our car was on springs instead of shock absorbers. I later realized that was exactly what had happened. Our shocks had completely ripped off the frame, and we were simply bouncing along on the springs. It also used as much oil as gas, and I had to put spark plug extenders on each plug to keep them from fouling out. It was obvious that the car was completely gone and not worth fixing, so I just called the scrap-yard and asked them to come pick it up the next day. Grace would be home, so I reminded her on my out the door for work the next morning that the tow-truck was coming out to pick up the car, and they would pay us fifteen dollars for it. We had rent due, and it would help.

When the tow truck arrived that morning, the driver handed Grace the promised fifteen-dollar check, and she exclaimed, "Oh I can't accept this much for the car. It runs and everything!" The driver laughed and said he would have to call his boss. He did, and in a few minutes he took the check back and handed her forty dollars cash. When I got home that night, I opened the door to see Grace jumping up and down in the kitchen with the forty dollars in her hands. We not only paid the rent, but we went out that night to our favorite Polynesian restaurant and got our favorite, the Pu Pu platter. What a life!

By the end of our first year of marriage, Grace had graduated with her education degree, and now I had one more year to go. In the spring of 1979 we moved to a much nicer apartment across town, and I found a better paying job at a large cabinet factory. The job paid for the higher rent, my tuition payments, and allowed us to buy another car. Grace was teaching at a small Christian school in the area, which also helped with our income.

Something else happened that last year that bears mentioning, especially in light of the plans we had been making. I had forgotten all about my freshman year's commitment to Canada and had been harboring thoughts of starting a new church in eastern New Hampshire upon my graduation. Grace and I had never seriously talked about Canada or Newfoundland for that matter. I think she thought I would just forget about my original intentions, and we would somehow live happily ever after not far from her family. One day on my way home from work, I began to think about those original impressions that had been made on my mind about Newfoundland that first year in college. When I got home, I went in my office and began to look through the letters I had sent and received with the Newfoundland pastor and considered what had really transpired just a few years earlier. That went on about a week before I finally realized that I couldn't get away from the thoughts of the "Rock," as the islanders call it. It seemed like all of sudden, I was hearing about this place in the north Atlantic everywhere I turned, and finally one Friday night after dinner at our apartment, I told Grace what I was thinking. She listened and smiled, but I knew she wasn't ready to say she felt the same way. Though she didn't know it, the next week at school was going to change that for her. About the middle of the week one of her young charges approached her desk asking her for help on his next assignment, which was a geography report on Canada. Not easily convinced by circumstantial evidence, she shrugged this off as totally unrelated to her particular dilemma and moved on through her day. She didn't even bother telling me about it that night. She did tell me that she was praying about our conversation the previous Friday night, but that was about the extent of it.

The next day, one of her favorite students appeared at her desk also asking for help on a new report he had to write. Grace asked him what he was assigned, and he just pushed his book to her to help him know how to pronounce the word, "New-found-land." Grace told me later that she nearly fell out of her chair. If Canada wasn't enough, the province of Newfoundland was enough to get her attention, especially coming from her favorite student.

On Friday night that week, we sat down for dinner, and before we finished the meal Grace began to tell me about her week at school. When she got to the "New-found-land" part she got tears in her eyes and in a few minutes we both were crying, then laughing. It was now a mutual conviction in both our hearts, and that meant we needed to inform her parents about our decision. After finishing the meal and cleaning up we headed over to her mom and dad's house to let them know what was happening. They took it with a similar sense of adventure that we did, but we knew that they would have loved to have us say we would only be a few hundred miles away rather than a thousand. We knew that they would support us, but it was good to hear it first-hand.

By the time graduation took place, we had already sent out a lot of correspondence to churches across the country who might be looking for an intern. We planned on working about two years or so under another experienced pastor before heading out to raise our support to go north. After a brief, painful stint in an Alabama church, we ended up taking a position with a church in the panhandle of Florida. We didn't know it at the time, but Grace was pregnant with our first child. Evidently, our term in Alabama had not been a waste of time after all. Less than a year into our internship in Florida, Allison Marie Snavely was born. She officially took the place of the Pekingese dog, Reuben (Hebrew for "Behold a son") we owned. God was beginning to give me the family I had always dreamed about growing up. Who would have ever thought that it would end up being my own?

We moved our family to Newfoundland in the summer of 1983. It took us two full weeks to eventually find an available apartment. Finally an apartment perfect for our needs opened up for us. Over the next nine years God would prove Himself to us over and over again as we began our church ministry there. Our family would also be blessed with two more daughters during our time in Newfoundland; Amy in 1983 and Ashley in 1986.

Early in the morning of February 16, 1990, my wife nudged me and told me to get up. She was going into labor. This was going to be our last child. We already had three children, all beautiful girls. When we brought Ashley home from the hospital, our neighbors chided us into trying again, as they had a few years back. Like us, they had three girls and finally got their boy on the last try. Never one to back down from a reasonably good challenge, I told Grace we at least owed it to our neighbors for the chance to have someone take the family name into one more generation. So here we were, leaving the girls with my mother-in-law and heading off to the hospital in our minivan. It was just a couple of miles to our city hospital.

Now, after nearly a decade of ministry, I had made scores of hospital calls here. But this one was different. I would be receiving, not giving. We pulled into the parking lot and slowly made our way into the admission area. We weren't really strangers around the hospital. Most everyone around there had seen one or both of us at sometime. Because Grace taught childbirth classes at this hospital, most of the staff already knew her from her being present at other births. Not only that, but we also ran "Family Bible Time" for several years on the local cable channel. It was always amusing to be standing in our neighborhood grocery store with local kids pointing at us while talking with mommy in hushed tones. I had also been contributing a weekly column to our daily newspaper for several years. Needless to say, we never could have been successful robbing banks in our town.

In just a few minutes they had Grace in the labor room, and I was at her side ready to coach her through the delivery. A few minutes later our obstetrician entered, apparently pleased to be involved in bringing our last baby into the world. She checked Grace and said she was making good progress and said she would check back shortly. It was just after eight o'clock in the morning. By the time she had checked back, it had become clear that this was going to be a marathon, not a sprint. Progress was slow, and this fourth child, if it was a boy or girl, was in no hurry to join us. About four that afternoon, it was time to meet our fourth child. The doctor told me to get on a gown and mask if I wanted to stick around. Of course, that was not even a question with me. I quickly got one on, secretly hoping the doctor would let me hold the baby right after it was delivered. I thought, if our doctor has a clue, she will at least offer. I had assisted with all three other deliveries even if was just cutting the umbilical cord. When I turned around to take my position at Grace's side, silently rehearsing the breathing patterns she would need, the doctor interrupted my thoughts by asking, "Bruce, what do you want to do on this one?" "Can I help catch it," I asked? She said, "How about you deliver it?" I thought she was kidding, but she wasn't. A moment later, I was poised to deliver my own baby while the doctor walked me through it step by step. I didn't notice it at the time but two other nurses were flanking me in the event I passed out or something. First the head was delivered, then a slight turn and the shoulder appeared, and then a whoosh and my rubber-gloved hands were immediately cradling a new human life. For a moment, I must have been in emotional shock. I was holding the baby face up, but the exhilaration was so great, I absolutely forgot to check the gender. At that moment, both nurses exclaimed in unison, "It's a boy," followed by yours truly a full two seconds later, "Hey, it's a boy!" For Grace, this final birth was the culmination of our family, and a love now twelve years old, that had blossomed between two young students in college. For me however, it was more, a lot more.

Not long after John was born, I was sitting down at my church office one day, and for some reason I couldn't get our housing situation off my mind. Actually, we had a nice house, which we rented, but that was the problem. We had rented this house for eight years and paid a small fortune on someone else's mortgage instead of our own. I don't know what came over me, but I told myself that this couldn't continue. I thought if my children were ever going to feel the security in life that I want them to have, they were going to have to have their own house that belonged to their mom and dad and not a landlord. Before I left the office that day, I got down on my knees and asked the Lord to somehow enable us to buy our own house. I had no idea how that was going to happen. We rented because we had absolutely no savings, and we lived from month to month on my small salary. I know it was small, because one time an auditor from Revenue Canada did an audit on our family finances. At the end of the audit he solemnly told me that I would be wise to consider taking a vow of poverty in order to help our tax situation. After he left, I told Grace what he said, and we both just howled. Neither of us or our children had ever thought that we were really that poor. We always had everything we needed.

When I got off my knees that day in July of 1990, I knew that something was going on, but I couldn't conceive of any possible situation wherein we could ever purchase our own home. Little did I know. About a week later, I had to speak out of town and needed to rent a car so I could leave my car with the family in my absence. A guy I knew who sold and rented cars lived up on the Trans Canada highway east of town. When I got to his house, I noticed he had a for sale sign in his front picture window. I thought that was odd, so after talking about car rentals I asked him why he was selling his house with a sign normally used for selling cars. He told me that a recently announced highway project was going directly through his property, and so he was being forced to sell. It was a well-built twelve year old, 2600 square foot ranch which was sitting on a cement-poured basement, but it would have to be picked up and moved to another location. He said the government had already paid him for the forced housing relocation, but he had two choices with the house. He could either let it be bulldozed, or he could sell it privately to someone who would move it. The removal date was December 1st, and he told me the price was $24,000.

On my way home I tried to conceive on how I could get his asking price in cash. By the time I got home I simply realized that without a loan, it wouldn't matter if it was $5000, I simply didn't have it, and without collateral, a bank loan would be out of the question. After I got back from my trip the following week, I decided to go out to a community about 10 miles east of town and have a look around. I had heard there was some building going on out there and I just wanted to have a look around. I drove around the small community of homes for a few minutes and then noticed an area of building plots, which had been recently excavated for building sites. I parked the car, got out, and began to imagine, if I could get that house, how I could get it into the area on the back of a semi house hauler. As I was standing there I noticed a diesel, dual-wheeled pick-up truck pulling into the site near me, so I asked the driver who owned the plots. He quickly said he did, and then asked me if I wanted to buy one. The real estate market was dead at the time, and nothing had been selling in the area for months, so I realized that he badly wanted to sell his plots to recoup some of his long-standing investment. I told him that I had a house I was interested in but needed collateral for the bank to give me a loan. I needed to finance its purchase, its relocation, and its reconstruction costs after settling it on a permanent location. He immediately realized that I was penniless and started laughing at me. Then almost as if he saw some kind of business opportunity in this poor minister, he said, "Get in your car and follow me". I got in my car and followed him around to a neighborhood on the other side of the residential area. We pulled up to a ten-acre plot that he had excavated himself and developed into about 15 separate lots along two parallel streets. He pulled along-side one of the lots, stopped and got out of his truck. When I got out he showed me a plot which had two stable and growing birch trees and was just a few hundred feet away from a wooded area which went way back into the bush. It was attractive and I began to wonder what I was even doing there. I didn't have any money, why even bother looking here? Then my excavator acquaintance told me the price was only $10,000 per plot, and then he said something that really got my attention. "What if I got my lawyer to draw up a legal draft putting the land in your name so you could use it at the bank for collateral?" Since the plot was right beside where he was building his own house, he said, "I won't have to go far to know where to find you if you don't pay me." When he made that brief, yet momentous offer, I somehow knew that God had just given me my house.

That next Monday morning I was sitting in the bank with my letter of collateral applying for a $55,000 dollar loan for buying, moving, relocating, and renovating the house once it was settled in its new location. The margins were close but the assessment value was greater than loan value, so by the middle of the week we were approved, and now the game was on.

The moving date was scheduled for November 1, and we would have to have all the permits in hand, along with a certified mover and driver no less than two weeks prior. I hired a guy from down in a bay town nearby who had a good reputation for moving houses and by the middle of October, they had begun to prepare the house for the six-mile move down the Trans-Canada Highway. The moving crew was a hard-living bunch who drank about as much as they worked, but they were experts when it came to moving houses. By the end of the month, they had the house unhitched from the foundation and sitting on the back of a semi truck ready to begin its journey to its new home.

Since all house moves had to be done on Sunday between sunrise and nine thirty in the morning, I told my church I might be late for the ten o'clock service. I purposefully scheduled one of our other capable teachers for the morning, so by seven o'clock Grace and I were parked out off the highway just across from our house. The movers were to arrive at no later than eight o'clock to begin the six-mile trek. At eight forty-five there was still no moving crew, but the electric and telephone guys had arrived to manage the moving of lines that might need lifted en-route. I was beginning to get worried when shortly before nine o'clock the movers finally showed up. We now only had thirty minutes to legally move the house, but they said they had to peel the only licensed driver they had off of his mattress, and he was really hung-over from a Saturday night binge. They told me not to worry, they had given him a few beers for breakfast and he would be good to go. I just closed my eyes, asked God to help him, and let the circus unfold. At this point I didn't have any other choice.

Our bleary-eyed driver hadn't been in the driver's seat for one minute when they all realized that the truck had settled down in the sod overnight and it was stuck right where it sat. When it appeared that hope was now gone for getting the move done by nine-thirty, I saw my excavator land-owner come roaring up in his Ford duel-wheeled diesel like he was the Lone Ranger on call. He must have sensed down at the site that something had gone wrong. His arrival was truly a spectacular sight. He turned around right in the middle of the highway, backed his truck up to the stuck semi and then hooked up to it with a cable. Jumping back in his cab, he waved at the driver to give it everything he had. All I remember is the roaring of the truck engine, which was overdone by the roaring of the diesel, and blue smoke pouring off the road surface where my excavator friend was almost lighting his big duel tires on fire in the attempt to pull the truck up out of the yard. In a moment, when the smoke cleared, we cheered from our van. He had successfully pulled the truck up onto the highway. In a few moments we were on our six-mile trek in the long caravan to the new location. If that wasn't spectacular enough, when we got to the site, the driver somehow managed to get the house on the exact specifications required by the city on only his second try, not bad for a bleary-eyed drunk.

For the next eight months, I poured myself into the basement renovation and all of the repairs needed to make the house whole again. Little did I realize that just nine months from the purchase of our home I would make another decision—to move on from our first ministry effort in Newfoundland. The newspaper sent a reporter out to our house the last week to get a personal take on our nine-year ministry in the city and our future plans. Since I had written a column in the Saturday edition for six years or so, it was a cordial interview. The reporter asked me what my first posting in this part of the country had been like. I distinctly remember telling her that I wouldn't take a million dollars for the experience. And with a wink I said, "I wouldn't do it again for a million dollars either."

Fortunately, we were able to leave a thriving church with some lifetime memories to take with us.

CHAPTER TWELVE

All the Way Home

WE TOOK A one year sabbatical in Virginia, and this allowed me time to assess some things in both our family situation and personal lives. I wanted to continue in church ministry in Canada, but I realized I needed to further my education along the way. I knew this would definitely affect my decision on our next strategic location. I also wanted to put my children in a private Christian school. By the summer of 1993, we had decided on relocating in Windsor, Ontario just across the river from Detroit. As it worked out, we were able buy a house in East Windsor, and matriculate our kids in a school across the border in Detroit. In fact, my wife was even offered a teaching position at the school. I was accepted at a nearby seminary in the area, and life immediately took on all the dimensions we had considered important while on sabbatical. We crossed the border every day, while starting a new congregation in East Windsor.

For the next five years, life was predictable, joyful,

and extremely busy. By the spring of 1998, my oldest daughter Allison was sixteen and ready to graduate from high school. She was two years ahead of her class by virtue of her home schooling in Newfoundland, and I was finishing my master's program right on time to graduate along with her from my seminary. Our family was poised for enjoying this truly, momentous family occasion.

Unfortunately, just before graduation week, we got the news that Grace's sister, home on furlough from Brazil had succumbed to cancer. We had actually known about the cancer but had hoped that after five years, she might have a chance to beat it, but unfortunately that wasn't the case. We were forced to leave town for her funeral just after I completed my master's defense at the seminary. It had been a little stressful, because I wasn't defending an academic thesis, but rather a doctrinal proposal. Although I was scheduled to graduate as an honor student, the seminary brass suddenly seemed unexpectedly resistant to a couple of minor doctrinal stances that I had taken in my defense.

Anyway, I thought little of it at the moment and got home just in time to pack our kids into the van to drive all night to Missouri for a funeral. We headed back from the funeral on Tuesday and drove all night. We got in sometime early Wednesday morning tired and emotionally spent, so we decided to just go to our friend's house in Detroit, shower and let the kids go to class from there.

When I knew someone would be at the seminary, I called the office to talk to the dean regarding the outcome of the previous Friday's defense and the next day's graduation. In a few moments I was patched into the president's office only to be told that I would not be graduating the following day due to disagreements the seminary had with my views on some very selective doctrinal issues. Despite my argument that to this point I had been a model student, mature pastor, and an academic honor student, the president told me it didn't have anything to do with these things, it had to do with the seminary maintaining its own doctrinal traditions in light of my differences. Even when I brought up mentors for whom he himself had worked alongside for years who held my exact opinions and widely held views, he was totally unaffected. It was unfortunate, he said, but told me "it was best for all involved."

I had suffered through some very difficult years as a young pastor in Canada, endured long seasons of loneliness, fruitless work, and tiring hours, but this was the toughest thing I had ever faced in my Christian experience. After a lot of counsel, prayer, and considerable debate with myself, colleagues, and the seminary brass, I decided my best course of action was to put it behind me and simply move on. I have long since recognized that this was one of the wisest decisions I ever made in my life. Later that summer, a ministry friend of mine called and asked me if I was interested in taking a course on the Dead Sea Scrolls at another seminary within driving distance. Knowing that I was still reeling from my previous educational experience, he knew that the best way to get me to move on was to get back into my studies. He then said, "This class is on me, if you decide to do it." Instantly I realized that I'd be crazy not to, so with some reticence, I decided to join the class. It turned out to be the best therapy I could have ever taken. Not only did I finish the class, but I enrolled for the following fall semester and transferred the maximum amount of credits from the other seminary. My academic advisor told me that I would have to complete thirty more hours that year to graduate, and so I decided to take the challenge.

To this day, I don't know how I managed to complete all those hours in seminary, pastor a small, growing church, and manage my family, but by the grace of God, it happened. In the spring, I was fortunate enough to be able to graduate with highest honors among my peers, and this time, with an actual diploma.

Sometimes, the best things in life are the hardest and take the longest, and my master's degree was no exception. I was probably the only guy in the country who had a Master of Divinity degree worth one hundred twenty-six credit hours. But just like my Newfoundland experience, I wouldn't take a million dollars for the experience, but I wouldn't do it again for a million either.

Just a few year's later, we made the momentous decision to leave our pastoral ministry in Canada for an administrative position at a college in Tennessee. Our first daughter was now in college, and our second daughter had been accepted at the college where I was to be working. My wife got a position teaching high school English and music at a local private school where my youngest daughter and son attended. Shortly after beginning my new position as Director of Recruitment,

I was also asked to teach part-time. I jumped at the opportunity and before long I was hankering for an opportunity to begin work on my terminal degree.

By the end of my second year I began to recognize that it would become necessary to begin looking for another teaching position for the following year. For no reason, my job description had been arbitrarily changed in mid-year, and despite a decent first year in recruitment, I had been forced out of my administrative post to teach exclusively. After a few months, I was informed that a Boston college was looking for a theology professor with a master's degree who would be willing to work toward a Ph.D, teach part-time, and then commit to five more years of full-time teaching after completion of the degree. Even though the job had already been advertised for a several months, I applied anyway and hoped for the best.

In late March, I was shocked to receive an invitation to come up for an interview; and to our surprise, I was unanimously chosen by the search committee as their Ph.D. candidate. So just a few days after our youngest daughter graduated from high school in May, we were back on the road again, this time to Boston. Back in March after getting the news from the search committee in Boston, I applied at two different universities, one in Chicago, and the other in Bristol, England. I had the privilege of taking a church history tour in the UK during my master's program, and I mused then that if I ever got a chance to do my doctoral work, I would do a research degree there. Little did I know I would get just that kind of opportunity. Fortunately, I was accepted at both, but decided on the University of Bristol. Research libraries in Bristol, Oxford, London, and Boston became my new passion for the next four years.

Now after completing my doctoral work and completing my five-year teaching commitment under contract, I have since left the college scene. Over the past few years I have started a new foundation for training church leaders globally. I have found that it completely satisfies both my academic passions and my desire to impact Christian service by helping to prepare those who will lead the next generation. It is thrilling to be able to give to those who serve their congregations or schools in the third world context the academic and practical training they never thought possible for themselves. After all, I have known some things which I used to think were impossible as well.

On our home front, all of my four children are now happily married, and they have given Grace and me six grandchildren to date with a seventh on the way. The family I always wanted continues to expand.

Now if you would have told me thirty-nine years ago that becoming a believer in Jesus Christ would have resulted in the life I have lived for nearly a generation, I would have probably thought you were absolutely crazy. But strangely enough, God really did have a plan for my young life. Even when I was that little six year-old boy peering over the edge of the casket of my father and kissing him for the last time, I could have never imagined that I would one day come to know another Father who would eternally embrace his orphan son. I could have never known then that this Father would give that boy everything he had ever wanted, including getting his family back, and ultimately make it possible to finally make it —*all the way home*.

EPILOGUE

Most of the names in this story have been changed to protect identities, but there are some individuals in the narrative for which you might like some closure. Lee's murderer, Gary Taylor, known better as the *Phantom Sniper of Royal Oak* continues to serve a life sentence for his multiple murders at the Washington State Penitentiary. He is now seventy-seven years old, and will never be released from prison. My sister's former husband Eric, after his divorce from Lee and release from prison, eventually re-married, went back to school, and went on to work with wayward children. Despite the years since the Viet-Nam war, he continued to suffer post-war trauma and passed away in 2001 from complications related to the condition. He was fifty-one. That same year Geoff, my brother, lost his life in a tragic car accident. He was only forty-eight and despite having returned to college, and earning his master's degree in bio-chemistry, he chose to simply paint houses for a living. He was in the middle of a painful divorce at the time of his death, and like our sister Lee, I don't believe he had ever been able to get beyond the past in his life. In my birth family I am the last remaining member.

At Geoff's memorial service, I was fortunately reintroduced to my half-sister Joan who interestingly enough, I continue a significant relationship with to this day. The only other member of my family still living at the time of this writing is my stepmother. She is in her ninetieth year. Unfortunately, we have no meaningful contact with each other.

My children are each married and doing well. My oldest daughter Allison and her husband Mike are franchise owners and have a thriving business near us. Allison is also an accomplished vocalist. They have given us three grandchildren: Braden, Macy, and Garrett.

My middle daughter Amy and her husband Todd are also both accomplished individuals who also presently live nearby. Todd has a master's degree in Biblical languages and Amy is a graduate of a music conservatory in Boston with a master's in vocal opera performance. She sings opera locally. Interestingly enough, they too are soon to be franchise owners like Mike and Allison. Todd and Amy have twin boys, Carson and Landon. They are presently expecting another baby.

Ashley, my youngest daughter has earned her master's degree in counseling, and is married to Lex, a film industry accountant in Toronto. Ashley is also a certified deep-muscle therapist.

Johnathan, my son is married to Rachel who is also

a beautiful vocalist. He is presently the district manager with a major Homes Systems firm, but is really passionate about his position as youth director at his local church. Johnathan was named after my father (who actually went by the name of John instead of Jeff). They have one child, Elliot Sullivan Snavely born in November, 2013. Elliot presently has the singular honor of carrying on the family name.

My wife, Grace, continues to be an amazing life partner and now, grandmother. We are enjoying our thirty-sixth year of marriage and are both excited about the prospects of watching our growing family continue to expand. We are partners, as well, in our non-profit teaching venture, Global Baptist Training Foundation.

If you are interested in seeing what the foundation is doing or where we are presently holding teaching sites around the world, we would be honored to make your acquaintance. You may reach us on our Facebook page or at gbtf.net.

Bruce Snavely, Ph.D
December 2013

ABOUT THE AUTHOR

Bruce Snavely is the founder and president of Global Baptist Training Foundation. After spending 20 years in ministry and 12 years in Christian higher education, Bruce's passion involves training national church leaders globally. He holds a Ph.D. in historical theology from Trinity College at the University of Bristol, UK. Dr. Snavely and his wife Grace have four children and seven grandchildren.